Who's doing who the favour?

What they still don't teach you in sales training

By James Bacon

Copyright not copyleft

ISBN: 978-0-9875847-1-7

18 months ago I found myself in an unusual position. For the past 10 years I had been training sales people and other professionals who sell, across the globe. I had consulted to some of the world's leading organisations such as "Googol", whose sales teams I have extensively worked with since 2007 across Europe, Asia and Australia. Yet for all of my experience and expertise I kept marveling at the predicament many sales people and their companies find themselves in. Today we know far more about selling and persuasion than we ever have. More people find at least a small component of their job involves selling and companies continue to invest millions of dollars trying to improve the quality of their sales people and the revenue each salesperson generates.

All of this poses an interesting question: why do so many people struggle to succeed in sales?

While I was convinced the answer would no doubt be long and complicated this question remained persistently in my mind. I felt compelled to investigate new and innovative approaches to sales. And you may not be surprised to learn that I found no shortage of gurus lining up to tell me how they, and they alone, had cracked the code.

Most, if not all, of these gurus had valuable things to say. Many of their ideas resonated and some of their models were very strong. Yet something still didn't sit quite right. In the flurry of arguments designed to convince me that Sales 2.0 (or whatever it was called) had finally arrived - and that I could forget everything I had previously learnt about sales - I started wondering whether we were looking in the wrong direction.

Perhaps the answer was not so much in big complex sales models as it was in the detail of our interactions with clients and customers - the 1% difference that is never taught in sales training. This notion caused me to reflect on the many coaching and training sessions I ran wondering why I was making a difference when many of my competitors weren't.

The penny finally dropped when my business partner posed the question to me: when we are meeting with a client, who's doing who the favour? All of a sudden the ideas came tumbling out of my mind, onto the computer screen and into this book. A collection of ideas, concepts and stories designed to help you regardless of your previous sales training.

I hope you find these ideas as helpful as they have been for me and I trust you have as much fun reading the book as I had writing it.

I'd like to thank...

My wonderful wife Nicola and my two gorgeous boys, Jack and Ben who make me feel so lucky every day. This family photo was taken just as I was finishing the book.

My mother and father for always being there for me, even when I live on the opposite side of the world.

My business partner Wayne Stewart for teaching me new things every day and for his support in writing this book.

The marketing team at Corrs Chambers Westgarth for challenging me to write these stories (or "James' Gems") in the first place.

9 ideas that will make a difference to how you sell

This book is focused on nine topics that I believe will make a big difference in how you sell and how successful you ultimately are:

1. Planning and preparation
2. Winning Relationships
3. Action speaks louder than words
4. Meeting clients and customers
5. Value is more than just price
6. Presenting and pitching
7. When the going gets tough
8. Teaming around sales
9. The 1% Difference

How you can use this book

I'm not one to be telling people how to read books, but I'd like to throw out a couple of ideas of how you could use this one.

Each page is a story in itself, so you could digest the ideas in bite sized chunks and simply read a page a day. The nine chapters in the book cover nine stand-alone elements of selling. Reading it one chapter at a time could be quite valuable. If you have the time or just love reading, take a chapter a day. For others perhaps a chapter a week.

It's my hope that some of the stories and ideas really resonate with you as "good ideas you'd like to start incorporating into your day to day selling". Highlight key points or make notes in the margin - it's a great way to quickly find and re-read the important parts. And don't forget the old fashioned way of simply taking the book with you to sales meetings and having a quick read in the taxi on the way to the meeting.

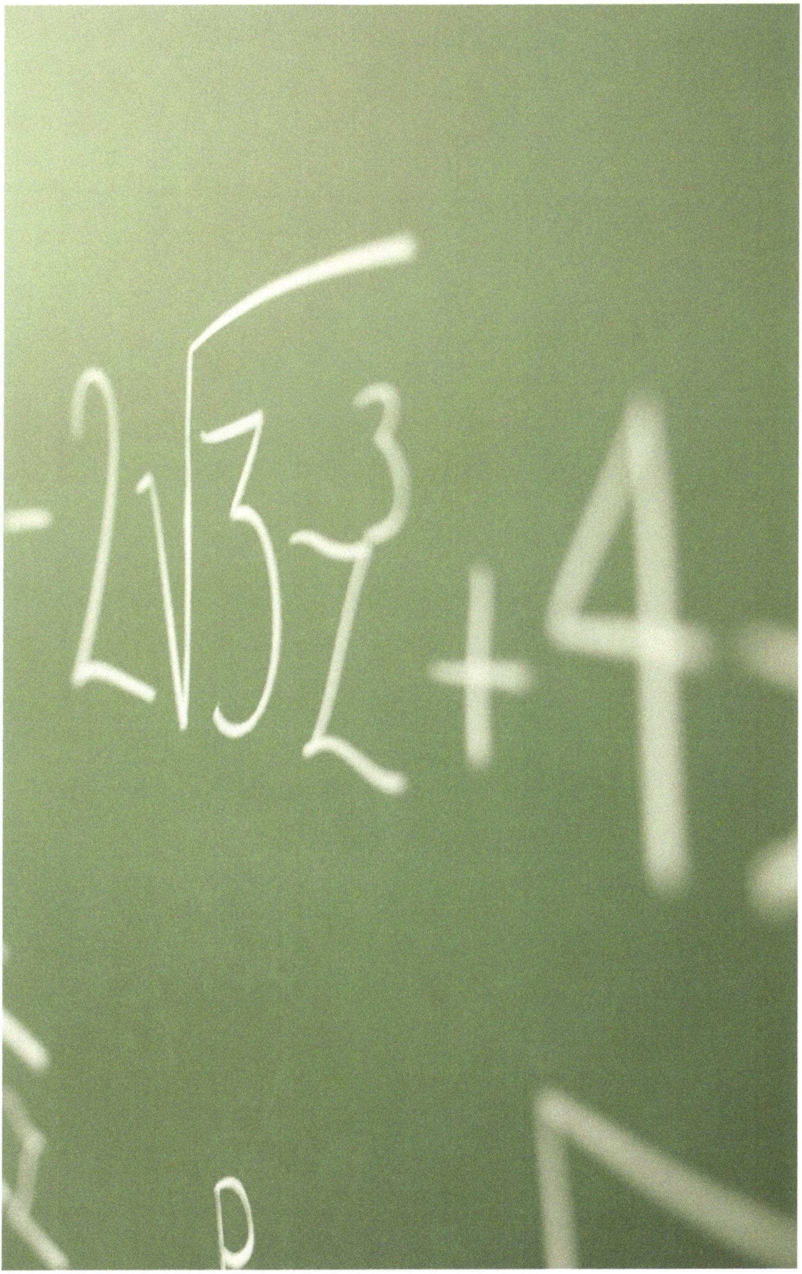

My dominoes for success

1. Have a mindset of giving not selling - giving value!
2. Relationships are never static - you need to continually invest and be thinking 'frequency of contact'.
3. Always start with the end in mind - for meetings, for networking, for presentations, for everything.
4. Focus your efforts with the right clients - not just the noisy clients.
5. Put time aside to prepare before any sales activity. Preparing and rehearsing is invaluable.
6. Structure your sales meetings, sales calls and sales presentations if you want the best chance of success.
7. Collaborate with your colleagues and don't try and do it all on your own. Selling is more fun as a team.
8. Always put yourself in the client's shoes. How would you respond to your call, your approach, your pitch?
9. Get in sync with the client and give them what they want, not just a sales pitch. The clients do the buying; you just help them brainstorm!

Get these right and the dominoes will fall in your favour.

Chapter 1:

Planning and preparation

"Always plan ahead. It wasn't raining when Noah built the ark."

- Richard C. Cushing

Who's doing who the favour?

The title of the book and a really important concept to understand. Imagine this scenario...you put a call into a prospective client and the decision maker agrees to meet with you. Now answer this - who's doing who the favour?

It is not unusual for the majority to think the prospective client is doing you the favour. Whilst we understand the client is giving up their time to meet with you, the answer needs to be "both". It's about making such calls and meetings "mutually beneficial" - with both the client and you getting value from it. This puts a different spin on 'selling'. So long as you have something of value to give the client, you are doing them a favour. Just this simple shift in mindset makes the idea of selling easier. Now you should be thinking "the client would be silly not to take the meeting".

9.63 seconds of glory

9.63 seconds is all Usain Bolt needed to win gold in the 100m in London 2012. With the weight of his nation on his shoulders, he performed in the heats, the semis and then the final. It was amazing to watch. What we'll never fully comprehend is the years of groundwork and training for his moment of glory.

Fortunately when selling we have more than 9 seconds to achieve glory: many meetings are 30 – 60 minutes long. Without the right planning and preparation Usain would not have succeeded. Likewise, we can adopt a small portion of Usain's gold-winning formula for our sales efforts:

1. Develop an agenda – how will you make the best use of the client's time?
2. Set yourself clear goals for the meeting – what outcomes are you looking to achieve?
3. Be clear on how you will contribute value to the client through the discussion – what insight are you bringing?

It would not surprise me if Usain Bolt, Yohan Blake, Sally Pearson and others also adhered to the credo of the 6 Ps: Proper Preparation and Planning Prevents Poor Performance.

Start with the end in mind

Pretty much the first question I always ask myself when planning for a phone call, a client meeting, or a presentation is, what do I want to happen AFTERWARDS. Do I want the client to agree to another meeting? Do I want them to agree to introducing me to someone else in their organisation? Do I want a "Yes, you have a deal"?

I find defining a clear outcome gives focus and helps with the rest of the planning. For example, what do I have to do, say and discuss during the meeting in order to have a realistic chance of achieving this outcome.

Many sales people don't do any pre-call or pre-meeting planning. I'm not advocating this is all you have to do, but simply clarifying in your mind the outcome(s) you want will give you greater chance of success.

Prioritising clients gives focus

Don't tell my business partner, but if I'm working from home I will often (always) get distracted. Distracted by a game of tennis, a round of golf or even the beach. We are all faced with distractions, especially when it comes to sales and business development.

Prioritising which clients to invest sales time on is important, as is the ability not to become distracted. It reminds me of the saying "he who shouts the loudest get's heard". When clients want, it is hard not to be distracted, not to turn your sales efforts to the noisy client, instead of the prioritised client. We suggest you start by prioritising your existing and target clients by the potential revenue they can give you and by level of effort involved in getting the revenue. The ideal focus should be on high revenue clients with relatively low effort. This way you'll see some quick wins as well as a solid pipeline.

Getting in sync with the client

What happens in a typical sales meeting isn't always what the client wants to happen. Too many meetings are focused on the seller not the client, meaning too much is centred on the capabilities of your company. This ONLY works when the client is in the process of picking a supplier. Outside of this, the client doesn't really care about you and the company's track record - because they already have a supplier. I'd suggest that for 75%+ of sales meetings, clients aren't interested in hearing about us, yet it's often our default.

The answer is to understand where the client is in the buying process and **align yourself with them**. You will rarely overcome incumbency by pitching your capabilities and experience. Instead, you win by bringing new thoughts, ideas, risks, opportunities, trends and lessons learned to the table. You win by discussing and debating potential risks and issues the client may or may not be aware of. Don't assume all incumbents are doing this – many aren't. I think it's time to give clients what they want.

Live for the moment

One fantastic surprise at the London Olympics was the Aussie men's K4 1000m canoe crew. Pitted against strong favourites from Europe the crew held a remarkable mindset: they accepted the strength of the competition yet still maintained faith in their own abilities. They knew if they put in their best race they would be right in the mix. The team understood their game plan and were thoroughly committed to it. Knowing your plan and implementing it can sometimes be very different things. In this case the Aussies concentrated their attention on the first 500m of their race.

Disappointment from missing out on the Beijing final was forgotten, any troubles with race preparation were set aside and fear about the strength of their opponents was replaced with a focus on their stroke and their tempo. They were truly "in the moment".

There is a great lesson here for how you sell. Planning and preparation are critical. Understanding the strengths and weaknesses of your competitors can be a massive advantage. From the moment you sit down in front of your client you need to apply your attention to the client, their challenges and their needs. By doing this you give yourself the best chance to win, regardless of whether you are the favourite or not.

14

Decision Makers vs. Decision Takers

In my early career I worked in advertising. I remember being given a large agency account to 'manage'. This meant ensuring they spent at least what they had committed to spending, but also getting them to spend more. Each week I'd have meetings with people at that agency...and how much did they spend? Exactly the amount they committed to, not a penny more (I was working in the UK at the time). Why - because I was talking to the wrong people. I was talking to the decision takers, not the decision makers. Big mistake. The lesson I learned was to identify and prioritise the different stakeholders in a company and allocate my sales time accordingly. That would be time well spent.

If you were the client, what would you do?

Knowing everything you know about your company's products and services, if you became the client tomorrow, what two to three things would you buy from your company and why?

This is a really interesting exercise to conduct when preparing for meetings. Answering it is not as easy as you think - it requires a really good understanding and knowledge of the client. But when you adopt this approach, I often see phenomenal reactions from clients. They love it.

Develop your two to three ideas as a one-pager to take to the meeting and share with the client. At worst you will have a great conversation and debate. Looking at things from a different perspective tells the client you are thinking about them.

Sales is not a marathon

You might have heard of the old saying "it's a marathon not a sprint". Well this saying doesn't apply to the sales race because sales is high intensity - often a campaign of short sprints.

Each time you meet with a client you are running a race and you are targeting an outcome. While you should aim to win every race you must also consider your strategy for the campaign of sprints you are undertaking. What are you building towards and are you getting closer to the ultimate gold medal?

Just like elite athletes you too should plan two, three or even four races ahead. Define the commitment you are seeking from the client in each meeting and check it against your ultimate goal. If you can't see the path to victory it may be time to change strategy.

Prepare for the worst and hope for the best

Mike Tyson summed it up nicely: "Everyone has a plan until they get punched in the face". There are many great quotes that highlight the importance of planning and preparation, but this is my favourite. Planning is vital in most things we do - coaching the local Under 11's soccer, an army General planning for war, a chef buying ingredients and yes, for those of us in sales.

So have a plan, but don't get constrained by it. Clients have their own plan most of the time, and you may need to 'bob and weave' (keeping the boxing analogy alive a little longer) to work with the client.

My suggestion is to plan for the worst and hope for the best. Think through the "what ifs" and have plans to fall back on. After all, you can't afford to get knocked out in the first round!

Fish where the fish are

One of my clients often gees up the troops by telling them to "fish where the fish are". I suspect he's telling his sales team to know where the good opportunities are and to focus on them. This may seem like an obvious statement but you'd be amazed how many salespeople end up fishing where the fish aren't. Everybody, and every company, has a sweet spot. Your sweet spot refers to the clients who love you and your products. Everything seems to go smoothly with these clients because they value what you bring to the table. In sales we want to extend this sweet spot as much as possible and the starting point for this expansion should be your existing clients. Take five minutes with each client to ask them why they buy from you, what keeps them loyal and what they appreciate about your relationship with them.

Once you have this list use it to evaluate new clients that you may be considering. Do they value the same attributes as your best clients? Be wary if they don't as you might be fishing in an empty pool.

The more you practice the better you'll be

Apparently Gary Player (the golfing legend) was practicing his bunker shots in Texas when this guy walking by stopped to watch. The first shot he watched, Gary holed it so he said "you got $50 if you knock the next one in". So Gary holed the next one. "OK, $100 if you hole the next one". In it went for three in a row. As he peeled off the bills he said "Boy, I've never seen anyone so lucky in my life" to which Gary replied "Well, the harder I practice the luckier I get".

It takes a lot of practice to become good at anything. Professional sports people, musicians, politicians (the list goes on) all spend hours practicing before they perform in front of an audience. Sales people don't always follow this rule. Often the first time we practice is on the client - which is never good. Time for you to hit the practice ground.

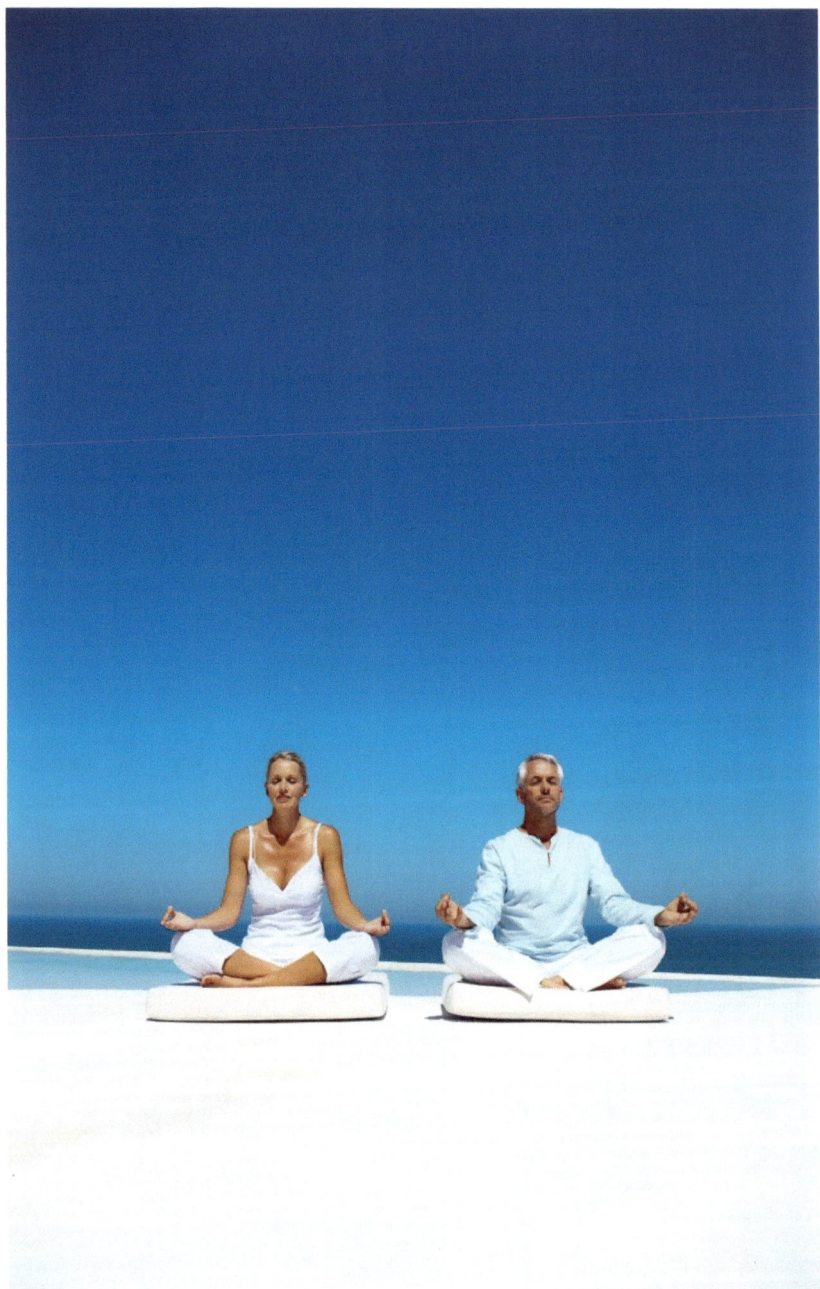

A great year; how about a great decade!

Most of us plan for the day ahead, or perhaps the week ahead. How about sitting down for just 15 minutes and planning for the year ahead - maybe even the next decade? What is your dream? Where do you want to be in ten years time? What do you want to have achieved?

To have a great decade (or even year) you need to turn your dreams into reality. This is unlikely to happen without you giving it the **necessary focus**. What do you need to do to achieve it? What processes do you need to put in place? What support do you need? What sales activity is required? Which clients do you want to be working with? And so the questions go on.

Now is the time to dream your dream. As the saying goes, "To accomplish great things we must not only act but also dream, not only plan but also believe."

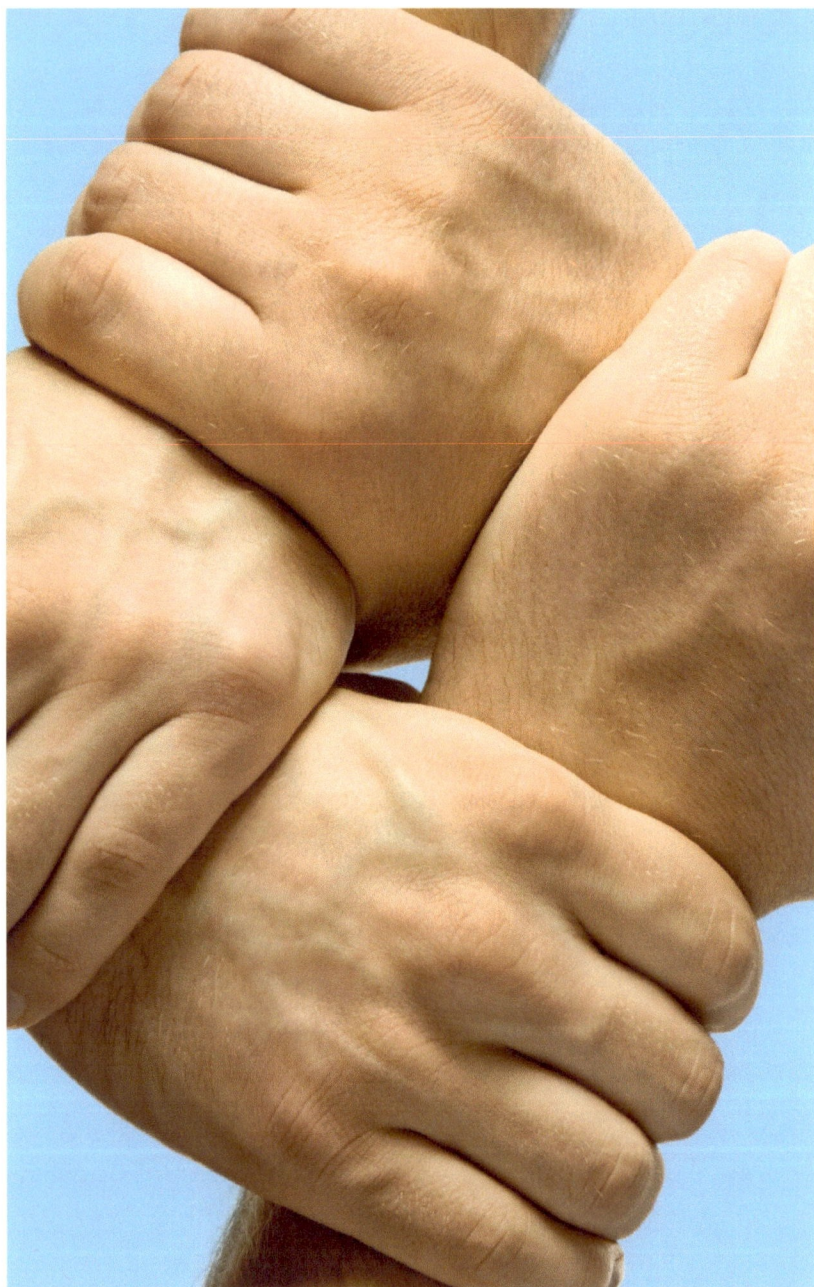

Chapter 2:

Winning Relationships

"Every morning in Africa, a gazelle wakes up knowing it must run faster than the fastest lion or it will be killed. Every morning a lion wakes up realising it must run quicker than the slowest gazelle, or it will starve to death. Either way, the gazelle or the lion, when you wake up you had better get running".

- Christopher McDougall

Are relationships everything?

Many sales people believe if they can build a strong relationship with a client that the work will flow. Unfortunately that's not the case. Relationships can make the difference between winning or losing work, but only when everything else is equal. And in the majority of cases, that's not the case.

That's why meeting for the sake of meeting is not enough, even when you know the person well. You need something to say, something to give, something that makes them walk away thinking "that was really worthwhile". It's this that will build the relationship more than the coffee and a friendly chat.

What have you got to say that will spark the interest of your clients?

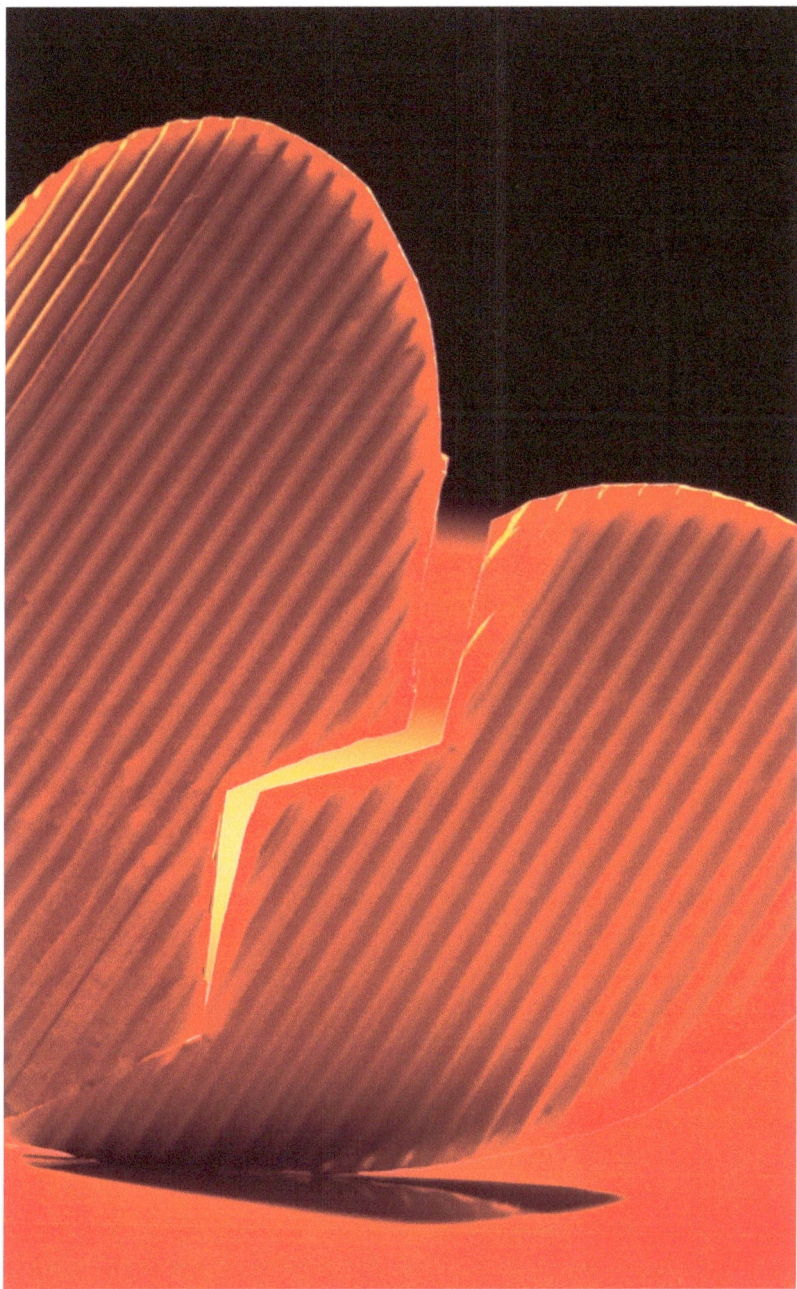

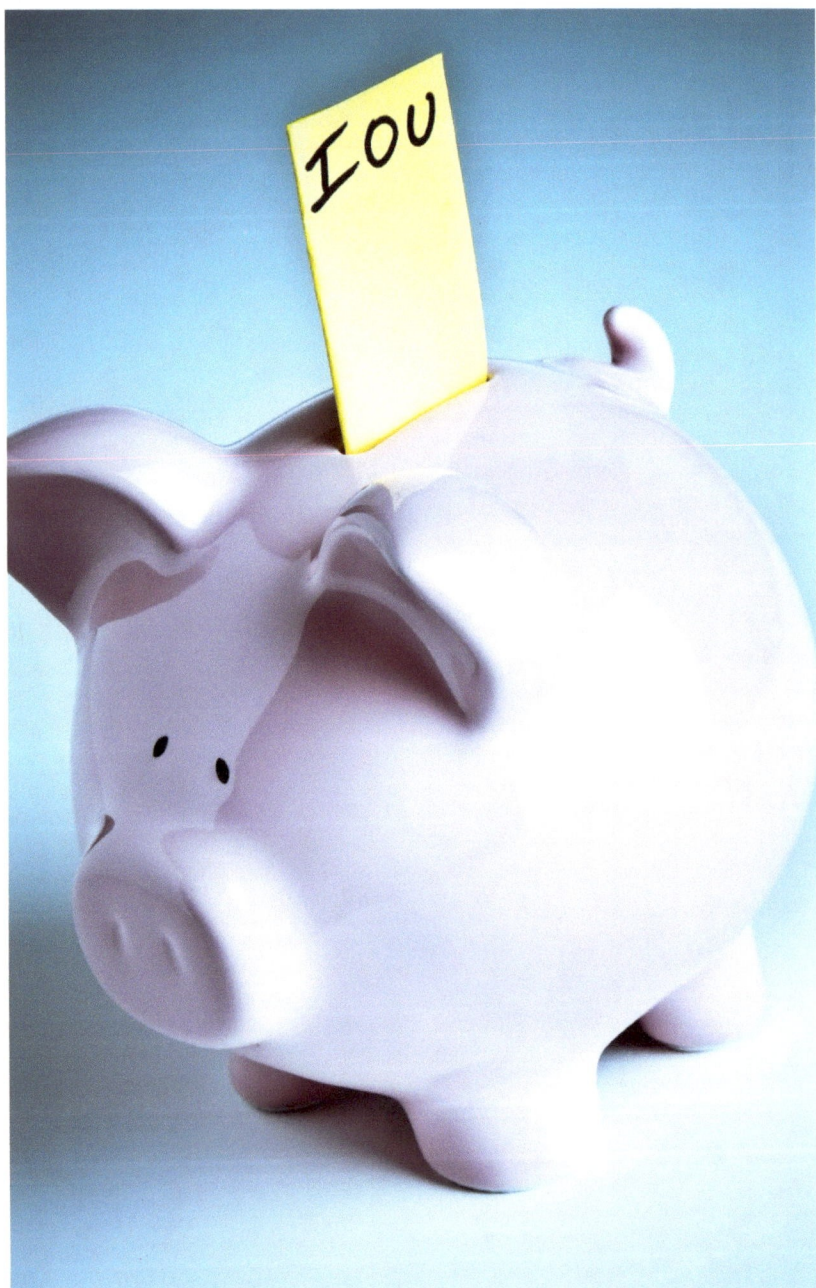

Building your emotional bank account

For those that haven't heard the concept before: you have an emotional bank account (EBA) with everyone in life - friends, work colleagues and clients. Your EBA works like your normal everyday bank account - you're either in credit or debt, but with individuals. You get credits for helping others, (delivering great work/service, acts of gratuity, going above and beyond) and debts for calling in favours. The more in credit we are the better - communication is effortless, trust levels are high, our ability to influence is high. Sounds good. We can't buy presents without money. Likewise, we can't (or at least shouldn't) ask for favors with no credit.

So spend time building credit with your clients. Look to connect them to other people that will be of benefit to them (not you), go that extra 10% servicing them - be super responsive, help them solve a problem, attend to the little things, keep to your commitments etc. Having a high EBA will stand you in good stead for the year ahead.

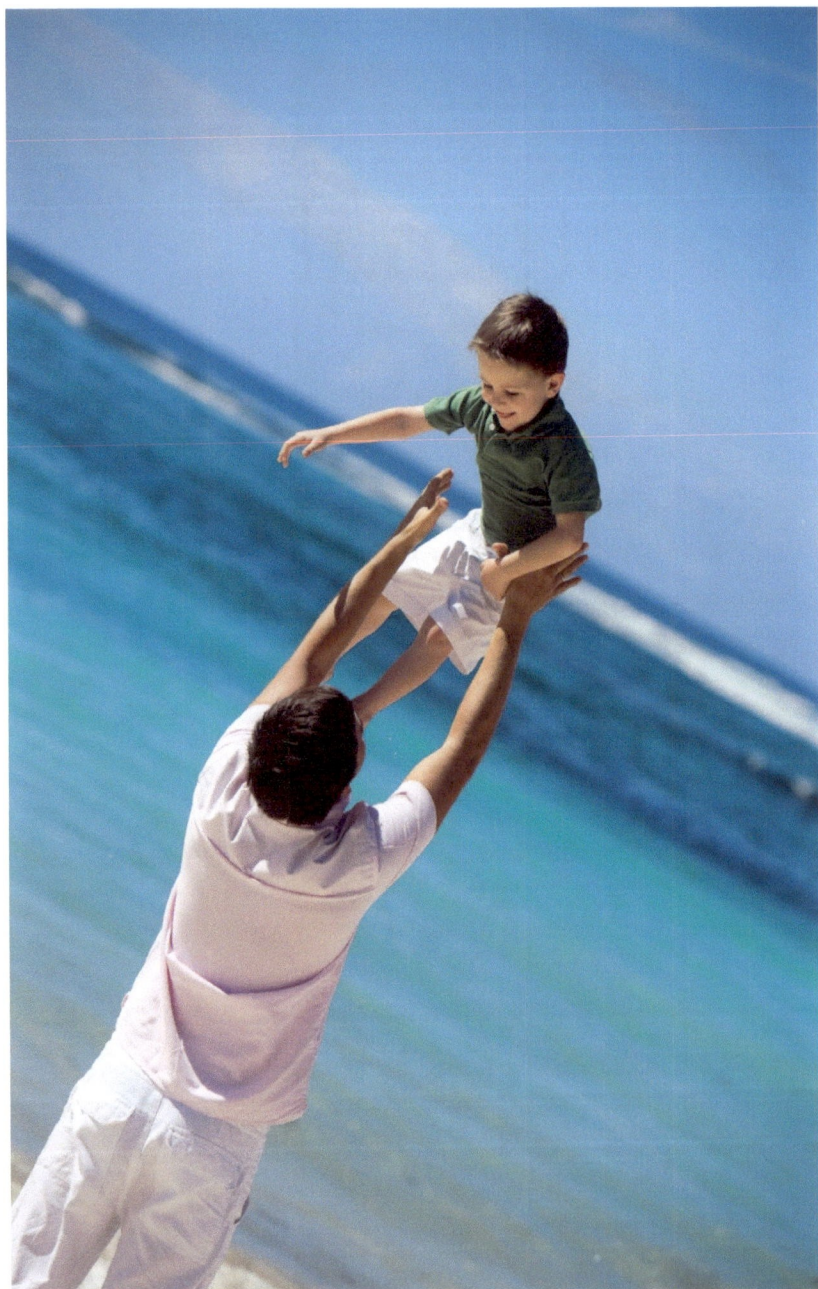

Frequency of contact matters

Every time I listen to the Simple Minds classic "Don't You (Forget About Me)" I'm reminded of this simple concept. How many people have you forgotten about? Former work colleagues, friends from university, former clients, current clients (I hope not)...people you haven't spoken to in over six months? For most of us it can be an embarrassingly long list, but don't worry - it's time to fix it.

Call them. Touch base. Say hello. Don't make it a sales call, it's a friendly call. If they suggest meeting for coffee, that's great. If they don't, that's fine - you've reconnected and when you call again in a few months it will be an easier call again.

I know the temptation is to leave it but the longer you leave it the harder it becomes to make the call. Who knows where these calls will lead...The point is regular call cycles are vital.

Relationship is not a one-way street

What I find most interesting is the definition of a successful 'relationship' in a sales context being **mutually beneficial** to both parties. I know many sales people where this unfortunately isn't the case. They invest heavily in a relationship yet get nothing back in return.

So what constitutes getting something in return? Ultimately the sale, but perhaps in the early days this is a little over ambitious. Often the simplest way to think about getting something back is ACCESS - getting access to decision makers and influencers within the organisation. Access to the right people gives you the best chance for making a sale, so I feel this is a two-way street.

Access is the key to trust

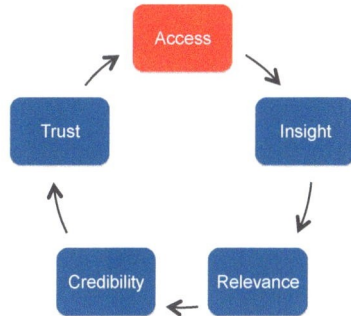

Outside of making a sale, getting agreement for another meeting is often the best outcome we can aim for. I call this access and access is key to selling. With it you are able to take insight to the client and in turn gather insight from the client (their current challenges, priorities etc). With insight comes relevance - you have now made yourself relevant to their business and as a result you establish further credibility. And with relevance and credibility comes trust, which in turn leads to further access. In essence this becomes a "circle of trust".

So make access a goal of every meeting and eventually even the client will trust you with their razor.

A boo is a lot louder than a cheer

According to Lance Armstrong, if you have 10 people cheering and one person booing, all you hear is the booing. Whilst it sounds tough, the principle applies in business as well.

Let's face it - not all your clients will love you. It's a personality thing after all. It doesn't mean they hate you, but means they like a competitor more, and that's ok. You can't be best friends with everyone you meet, so don't try to be. People buy people, so stop thinking you have to own all the client relationships. Keep doing what you're doing with those clients that love you, but look to introduce someone else (from your team or the company) into the relationship...someone the client will love. Now clients will love you for doing that!

Avoid the single buyer trap

There is easy selling and there is strategic selling. Easy selling has you contacting and meeting with your list of 'usual suspects' - those clients/prospects you know reasonably well and can get in front of without too much difficulty. Don't get me wrong - this is good sales activity, but it's easy.

Nowadays multiple people from the client side are involved in the decision process. It's rarely just one person (even if that's what they tell you). Having one supporter is rarely enough. Which means you have to broaden your relationships and go higher and wider. Map out the likely decision makers and get to work - because if you're not, someone else is.

I now pronounce you husband and wife

Many of us spend a lot of time looking for Mr/Mrs Right. Given we spend as much time at work as we do at home, why don't we apply the same Mr/Mrs Right rules with our clients? I often hear "they are a difficult client" or "they just aren't nice to deal with" and I wonder why you stay in a relationship like that?

Life is too short to work with clients you don't like. So either work with the client to fix the relationship (it has to work for both parties) or find another client to replace them. If we get the ground rules right, we'll both live happily ever after.

You have to give in order to get

The biggest problem sales people have is they believe they are there to sell. This is flawed. Immediately you focus on what you are selling, you lose focus of the customer - and that can't be good. Add to this the fact that no-one likes being sold to and we have a problem.

The answer is to **start giving** and stop selling, especially in the early sales meetings.We all have things to give customers - some ideas, some insight into the market or a competitor, a sense of what the future holds, forewarning of possible risks and problems and so forth. Customer's value all of these and you'll suddenly find giving becomes your best form of selling.

Sometimes "no" is better than "maybe"

At a previous consulting firm we used to call them 'see mores', clients that always wanted to 'see more' stuff, but who would never buying anything. Things like "can we see bio's of the whole team?"(action for us, not them) or "can you provide some references of where you've done this before?" (more work for us, nothing for them). Eventually they would inform us they were going to do the project internally! It taught me a good lesson: often **clients don't like saying "no"**; they prefer "maybe". It's easier and it obviously avoids the conflict of saying "no". Maybe's are not good for us though. We end up investing too much time with prospects that have no prospect! My mantra is "if you're going to get a "no" get it sooner rather than later", which means you have to make it easy for the clients to say "no" . Take the pressure off them and maybe you'll get the truth.

It's not what you do; it's how you do it

Differentiation can be tough in today's market. Is your company better than your competitor? I'm sure you'd like to think so, but making that distinction to clients can be tough. Often clients take what you do for granted - for example there are hundreds of accountants who can do the job. It's how you do it that really matters.

For me, you need to be going "above and beyond" with your clients; with existing clients to ensure they have no interest in talking to a competitor; with new clients to demonstrate what you'll be like to work with should they choose you. Look to give clients the same service levels and care everyday, as if it's your first day working with them. Because as soon as you drop your game, your competitors are in with a chance. Above and beyond every time!

You are the Sherpa and the client is the Explorer

A simple but useful analogy for sales people is to look upon themselves as a sherpa, whose job it is to guide the client to the summit of the mountain. This is one of the reasons we chose the name 'Monte Rosa' for our business - I liked the concept of helping clients reach their summit. The summit can represent many things - increased revenue, reduced costs, advantage over their competitors, a more loyal workforce and so on, all a direct result from using your products or services.

You can't push the client up the mountain - they must climb of their own volition. But you can guide them, helping them avoid potential issues and helping them choose the right path. And this is the role of the sherpa. Are you up for the challenge?

Be Tenzing Norgay

The man needs no introduction...or does he? While Sir Edmund Hilary is the person most famous for first climbing Everest, Tenzing was the faithful Sherpa (or trusted advisor) who ensured Sir Edmund's goal was achieved.

As sales people, we should try to emulate Tenzing, helping our client's navigate difficult (and often treacherous) situations when there's a lot at stake.

1. Support the client: ensure everything runs smoothly and keep them aware of unrecognised risks that may impact success
2. Motivate the client: keep the client focused, on track and up-beat, especially at tough times
3. Push the client: doing nothing is the easy option
4. Pull them back: to ensure they don't make rash decisions or mistakes

If Tenzing can get Sir Edmund to the summit under such adverse conditions, I'm imagining your journey should be somewhat easier!

A different direction

Not the leader? Not a problem.

Two sales people are walking along the beach one day when they come across a crocodile. The croc bares its teeth and readies to attack them. The first sales person turns to escape and realises his colleague has stopped to put on her running shoes. "You're crazy" the first sales person says, "you'll never outrun that croc!". "I don't have to" she replies, "I just have to outrun you!".

Sometimes we get so wrapped up in the strength of our competitors that we lose sight of the truth that each client buys from the supplier **who they believe** will best meet their needs. It doesn't matter if you've lost the last five deals to your arch rival. If you do a better job of uncovering, developing and meeting the needs of your next client, your chances of success will sky rocket regardless of who you're up against.

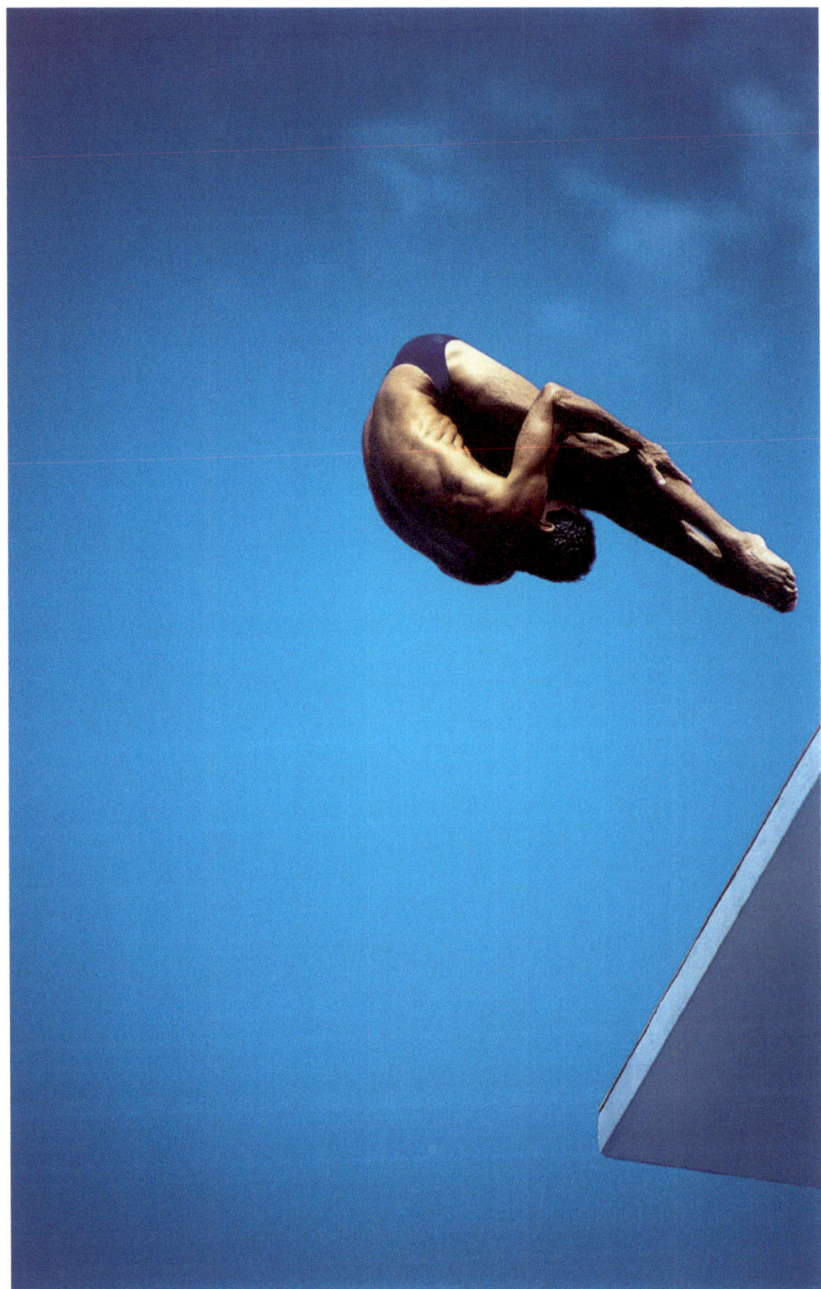

Chapter 3:

Action speaks louder than words

"You will learn more about a road by travelling it, than by consulting all the maps in the world."

- Unknown

It's not rocket science. It's discipline and energy!

There are some things in life we know we are supposed to do, yet often don't - like drinking eight glasses of water a day; eating your five-a-day fruit and vegetables; and exercising three times a week. I'd also like to add business development to the list. You know you need to do it. You know you can't afford not to do it. And yet, we often don't do it (or at least enough of it).

So what is the magic number of sales activities a week? I think it will depend on your job and on what you're selling. If you're looking for a guide though, observe your high achievers in the office - they've often got it right.

Being proactive wins the hearts of clients

The constant moan I hear from clients (not mine of course!) is that their current suppliers are not proactive enough. Clients don't like it when the only time you call is because you have seen a reduction in their spend levels or because there is a problem that needs resolving. Clients want you to be proactive with them - to look for opportunities, ideas or potential issues on the horizon. If you read something that will interest them (even if it's outside of your field of expertise), send it to them. It doesn't always have to result in a meeting - a phone call is often enough or sometimes an email with the link to a relevant newspaper article or piece of research.

You actually have nothing to lose. Even if the client says "thanks, but it's not of interest at the moment" at least they know you are thinking of them and 'care' about their future.

Let's get visible, visible. I wanna get

Inspired by Olivia Newton John's famous song, we don't need to get physical - we need to get visible!

If you want internal referrals, sitting at your desk doesn't work. Neither does sending emails. You need to walk the office floors, pop into people's offices and engage with them - and ask how you can help them before how they can help you.

Externally the same applies. You need to be active in the market. Sitting in your office waiting for the phone to ring is a poor strategy after all. I find the more visible I am, the more work seems to come my way.

I believe it's not what you know that counts, but who you know and who wants to know you and it seems that principle applies to internal as well as external relationships.

Don't stop me now, I'm having such a good time

Every book needs reference to a Queen classic to inspire action. Here is mine. There are always quiet periods in the year. Many businesses shut down for 2-3 weeks over Christmas (in Australia it's even longer). School holidays, Easter, end of financial year...there are many times things slow down, but that doesn't mean your sales activity has to.

Two suggestions for you: firstly schedule a range of sales activities for when the 'silly season' is over. You really need a pipeline of sales activity to return to rather than an empty diary. Second, not everyone is away at the same time. Use these times to arrange coffees/catch ups to discuss the coming quarters - their goals etc. Getting ahead of the game is important and now's your chance.

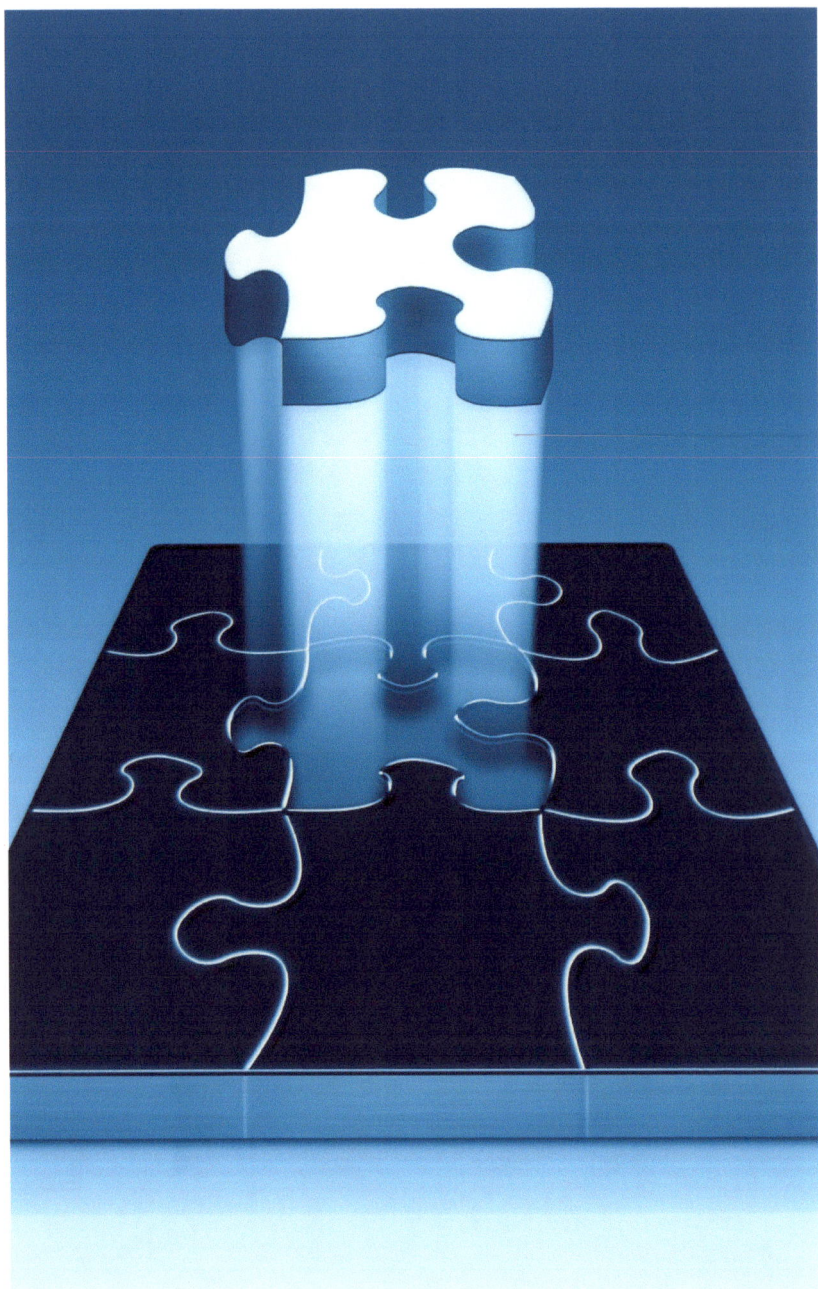

Imagine if you did everything you said you would do

I read somewhere that "those who are blessed with the most talent don't necessarily outperform everyone else. Those people with follow-through are the ones who excel". I'm sure the person that said this wasn't aiming it at sales people, but they should have been.

In short, sales is about execution, action and follow through. Try to set time aside every day to get through your sales activities, even if it's just time to make some phone calls or schedule some meetings.

Knowing what to do is rarely the problem - it's doing it that is hard. So try not to let your sales activities fall to the bottom of your To Do List. Instead be inspired by Nike's slogan, and "Just Do It".

Chapter 4:

Meeting clients and customers

"Accomplishment will prove to be a journey, not a destination."

- Dwight D. Eisenhower

Rapport - too much or too little

Most people believe building rapport is an important element when selling. I agree. However, while many do it, many do it badly. People fall into a couple of traps - spending too little or too much time on rapport or seeing rapport as idle chit-chat at the start of the meeting. Here's how to avoid both:

1. Rapport should be between 2-10 minutes long. Any less is not enough, any more is too much. The key is not how much or little rapport you want, but what the client wants. Be guided by them. Rapport building needs mutual interest. If the client isn't reciprocal in asking you questions, take that as a signal to commence the meeting.

2. Rapport isn't talking about the weather or the latest news and sport. Rapport is about finding commonality, something that interests both of you. LinkedIn gives you the background and experience of the person you're meeting and perhaps you can weave these nuggets of information into the rapport piece.

The overarching message is be guided by the client initially, but don't lose sight of your end goal.

From small talk to business talk

The transition from small talk to business can be difficult. How long should one spend on small talk? We know it's important but some clients seem happy for us to keep it going...before telling us our time is up and disappearing into another meeting and leaving us having achieved nothing. So what's the answer?

"Ok, enough small talk. Let's get down to business" is not really appropriate. So instead:

1. Transition from small talk (personal) to business small talk (about the industry, competition). This makes transitioning to the actual meeting easier

2. Use an agenda - this can be shared with them beforehand in order to have them contribute to it. That way they have a vested interest in getting down to business - in fact they may even move the conversation along for you.

3. Clarify the time you have - "Sorry Tony, I'm very conscious of your time. You said you only had 30 minutes and there are a couple of ideas I'd like to get your thoughts on."

All you need to know can fit on the back of a business card

A good friend of mine recently retired having established and sold two successful recruitment businesses. He is what we'd call a 'natural salesperson' with great intuition learned over 25 years of selling. However, unlike many natural salespeople, he can articulate what he does and we have heard him coach his recruiters explaining "everything you need to know can fit on the back of a business card". This is how it goes:

1. Build rapport (5-10 mins)
2. Understand the client's needs (20 - 25 mins)
3. Summarise your understanding of their needs (3 mins)
4. Present and discuss your solution (15 - 20 mins)
5. Close (5 mins)

It's pretty straight forward, but I like it's simplicity.

Slow down for yellow lights

So you're in your car and the traffic light turns yellow. What do you do? Do you hit the accelerator or brake? In meetings we are often faced with the same scenario. Clients often say things that represent a yellow light - things that don't seem quite right, low expectations around what it will cost, who is/should be involved in the decision making process, lack of awareness of the complete issue etc. Whatever it might be, it constitutes a yellow light, and we need to slow down, not accelerate.

Sales people are often afraid of losing the opportunity and 'feeding it rather than killing it'. Ultimately if you're going to get a no, surely it's better to get it sooner rather than later?

So look out for yellow lights. Listen to what the customer says and how they say it (body language, tone etc). Anytime something doesn't feel right or you feel concerned, raise it with the client. There's no point running a yellow light and getting caught by the speed camera. It's points on your Sales License and clients should hit us with a fine for wasting their time as well!

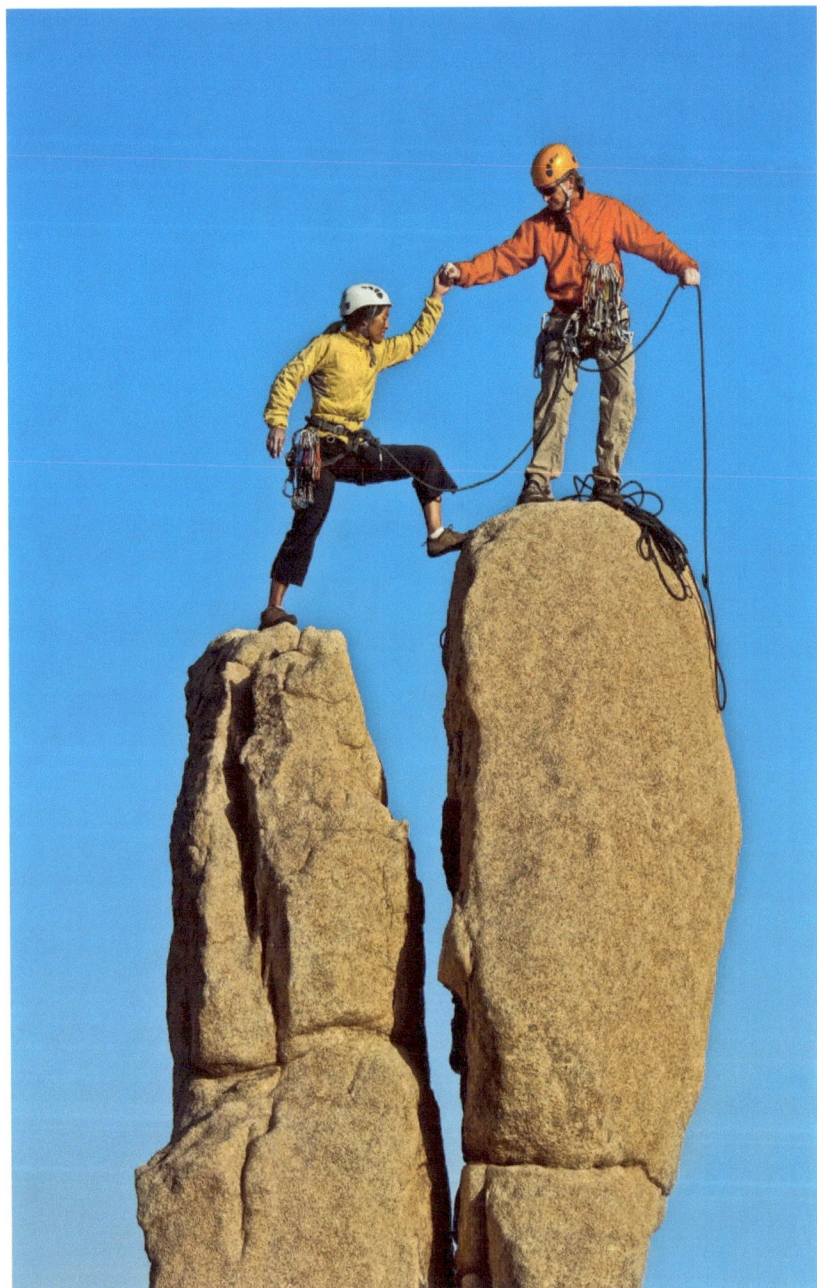

Selling to the C suite (C'X'Os)

I heard a statistic recently that stated there were 417 sales professional for every one CXO in the US! 417 to 1 - wow! Whatever the ratio is in your country, I imagine it will be heavily skewed towards sales people, so what does this mean?

It means we need to have a really compelling reason to get access to CXOs. These are busy people who don't like being sold to and whose diaries are often carefully controlled by a personal assistant. Carefully consider your 'hook' for the meeting. If you were them, would you take the meeting? If not, go back to the drawing board and don't waste your one chance in front of them. When you do get in front of them, make sure you have done your homework - go armed with an understanding of their business and their issues and use the time with the CXO to confirm your understanding and then discuss how you can help them succeed. They aren't interested in your product, but they are interested in what it will do for them.

Friends are there to help you - use them!

My wife is looking to get back into the workforce having had time off bringing up our two boys. She is going to help launch a new approach of ours, Sales Gym. What I find interesting (and a constant debate between us) is her unwillingness to use her friendlies (social friends or people who think favourably of her in a work context) for help. She says they aren't decision makers. I say that's fine, if they were, great, but if they're not, they can still help. So how can friendlies help? **Information, introductions and access**. Friendlies are typically receptive to giving you information (current focus of the company, key challenges, people you need to talk to etc). They can also facilitate access to these decision makers or simply let you mention their name. So go and talk to your friendlies and look at LinkedIn to see your friendlies' contacts - I bet there is a friendly lead in their list!

Dont talk - just listen (and then some)

There is an expression "people don't like being sold to, but they love to buy". For clients, talking at them equates being sold to and listening to them means buying - and it's much easier if they want to buy!

Part of this means we have to be good at asking questions. I bet if we surveyed sales people around the world right now we'd probably discover that about 50% have absolutely no idea what questions they're going to ask the client; 40% would have a general idea and only 10% would have a good idea. Of that 10%, only 1 in 10 probably has a written list of questions. Amazing!

It's tough to ask good questions off the top of your head. Perhaps it's time to put together your own check list of questions. Whilst you'll have to tweak them for each meeting, you'll have done 90% of the hard work already and you should notice a big difference in the quality of your meetings.

Listening to learn; learning to listen

"How did you learn all this?" I asked. "I asked a lot of questions" he replied. "Right, I'm going to ask more questions" I said. "No, that's not the answer" he said, stopping me. "I asked lots of questions AND I listened to all the answers".

Much has been said on the topic of talking and listening, probably too much! Sales people have been told that asking questions is the key to success and clients now spend many hours answering sales people's questions often for no perceived benefit. Don't get me wrong - engaging clients through questions is a vital part of selling, but the key is asking the right questions and listening carefully to the answers. If you could only ask the client ten questions, what would they be? Selling requires balance - balance between you asking questions, listening to the answers and providing information. Only when you get this balance right will success come.

Listen with your eyes and your ears

Yes, get your senses working when you are selling. You are looking and listening for buying signals - signs from the client that they want to buy from you, or hear more about your product or service. The problem is a lot of sales people miss these signals and instead keep asking questions or transition the conversation somewhere else. Listen out for signals such as "what would you recommend, how could you help us, tell me more or I like the sound of that". These statements provide us with a natural transition from questions to discussing a solution. At the same time, you need to be looking for positive signals. Watch the client's body language - often clients will lean forward to indicate interest, their facial expressions will change and they will typically relax more.

Reading a client by what they say and their body language is an art. Try it in your next meeting.

Open or closed - that is the question

I love playing and watching tennis. The game has certainly become more of a baseline battle than it used to be in the days of McEnroe, Becker, Rafter and Sampras, with today's points being longer and the players having more time to construct the point. Similarly, I like to think of open questions (those that generate a broad response) as playing on the baseline. Here you and the client have time to question and answer and enjoy the rally. Closed questions (those that can be answered in one word, often yes or no) I liken to coming to the net - you have less time before the ball is back in your court. No sooner have you asked your question, you have the answer - and back to you. You actually put yourself under greater pressure with closed questions and whilst there is a time for them, I'd recommend you try to stay open.

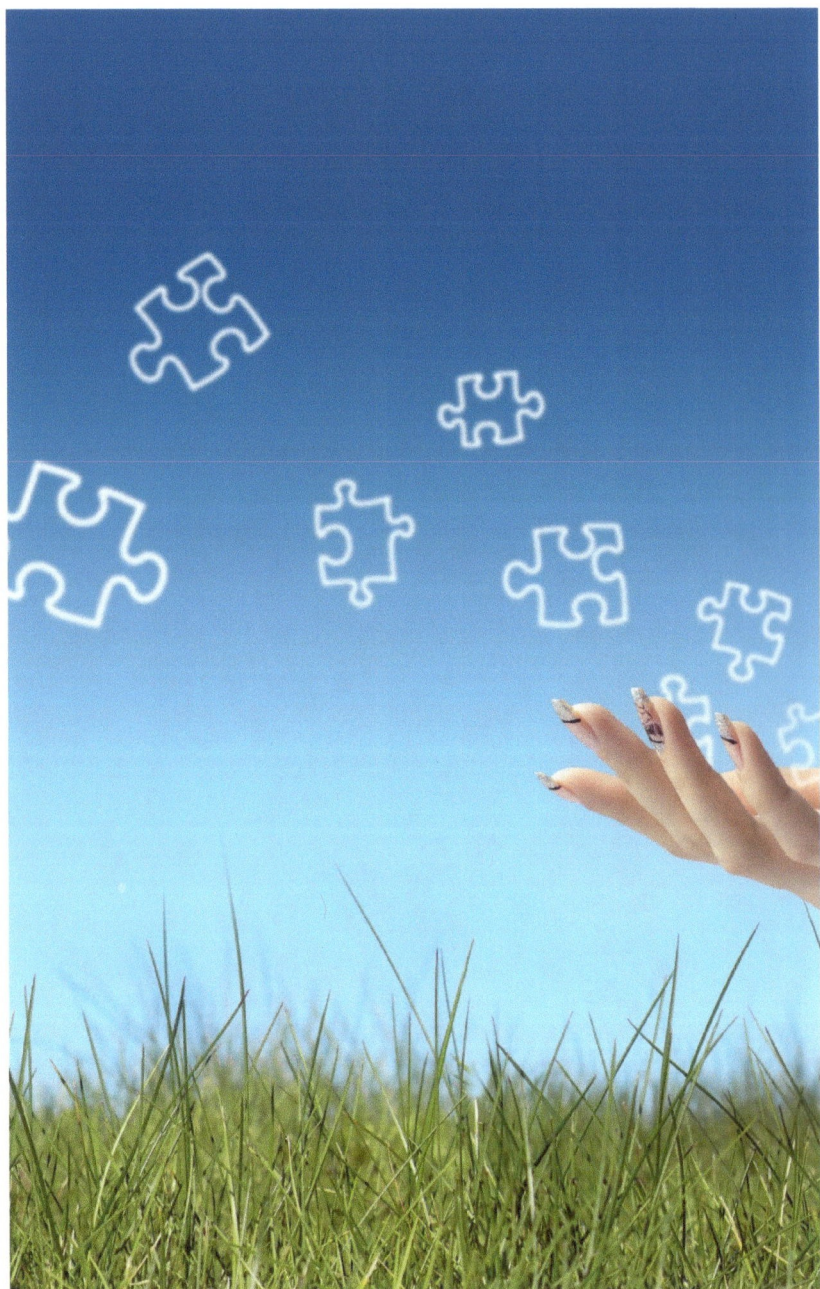

If, when, why, what, how much have you got?

This was a line from the Pet Shop Boys' classic "West End Girls". Whenever I think of asking questions, in particular open ones, this phrase always springs to mind. Here are a couple of tips for ensuring you ask more open questions:

Firstly, write down the (open) questions you want to ask the client in advance. Whilst I'm not suggesting you read them from the page during the meeting, just thinking of the phrasing and writing them down will give you a better chance in the meeting.

Next, on the top of my notes page I write down "how, what and why". Simply having these words in front of me gives me the starting word for all my questions.

It's a little like an actor rehearsing their lines and these tips for me are just another piece in the puzzle.

What you can learn from your local GP

When you visit your local GP/Doctor and explain your ailment, rarely does the Doctor prescribe the medication / solution immediately. Instead they ask a range of questions to better understand how it happened, when it happened etc.

It's a simple analogy, but too often I see sales people dive into a solution without properly diagnosing the issue.

I think it's time we all adopted the Doctor approach. ONLY when you understand the perspective / issues / needs of the customer as well as they do should you be discussing the solution. Even if you have seen the same issue with another customer, every customer likes to feel unique and the journey of diagnosis creates this sense of uniqueness.

To assume - to make an 'ass' out of 'u' and 'me'

You have probably heard it before, but I think the point needs reiterating. How many assumptions do we make every day about our clients? Too many, that's my guess. We assume things about their business, about them, about what they are thinking, about what they want and so on.

My advice is "No Assuming". Instead, take time to clarify your assumptions with your clients - you will learn more and make less mistakes.

The key is to "never assume the obvious is true" and "assume nothing, question everything".

Clients want an enjoyable experience

Rightly or wrongly Mel Gibson gave us an insight into what women want. Wouldn't it be great to have similar insight into what clients really want? Well here it is. Apparently they want a high quality product or service. No surprise there. What they also want is an enjoyable sales experience. Now that's interesting because we rarely take that into account when planning our sales meetings.

This raises the question - how can we make the sales experience more enjoyable for clients? Here are two ideas:

1. No-one likes being sold to, so stop selling to clients and start helping clients

2. Make it all about them and not about you. Clients are fed up with sales people talking about themselves and about their company...but like talking about themselves!

CHAPTER 4 - MEETING CLIENTS AND CUSTOMERS

Is a coffee ever just a coffee?

Coffee seems to do strange things to people... aside from keeping them awake when consumed late at night. Take sales meetings for instance. With coffee we feel compelled to make our conversations organic as we're terrified of looking obvious or contrived in front of a client. Any thoughts of developing a goal for the meeting or setting an agenda fly out the window as we try our utmost to look cool and relaxed. Suddenly the meeting has a subtext that frequently the sales person and the client find difficult to read. Life wasn't meant to be this hard.

With coffee the issue keeping us awake at night, aside from the caffeine, is one of permission: is the client ok with us turning the conversation towards business? The most effective solution here is also the simplest – ask the client if they'd mind us talking business. If you're worried that the client presumed this is merely a social catch up then suggest another meeting when you can sit down with them in their office, without beverages if need be. Keep it simple and straightforward. Clients will appreciate your honesty and you'll find your sales goals become much easier to achieve.

It's as easy as ABC - or is it?

A - always; B - be; C - closing: Always Be Closing. Alec Baldwin delivered this line as part of a seven-minute 'pep talk' to a bunch a under-performing estate agents in the film Glengarry Glen Ross back in 1992. It's been viewed over 4 million times on YouTube and I imagine is a favourite with sales trainers around the world. The question is, is it the right approach?

I would actually say "not". I believe there is a time and a place to close, but closing at the wrong time puts undue pressure on the client and breaks rapport, hence the timing is crucial. Closing is a natural part of the sales process and it happens towards the end of the meeting/call, once you've asked the right questions, understood their needs and then tailored your solution to meet these needs. This momentum you've created is important. At this point (and only at this point) the client is ready to buy and so closing becomes easy. So closing is as easy as ABC, but perhaps not in the way Mr Baldwin suggests.

Collateral damage

As much as I enjoyed the Arnold Schwarzenegger film, this is about marketing collateral and the improper use of it. Sales people love it. It's their crutch or support. Some pull it out at the start of a meeting, some during and if they haven't produced it by the end, out it comes before they say farewell. At the start of a recent sales meeting the prospective client asked me if I had prepared something or had a brochure I'd like to talk through in the meeting. I replied I didn't. I stated instead I wanted to spend the time discussing their business, challenges, opportunities and desired goals and explore different options before I tabled anything. "Thank goodness" was the reply. "The last consultant came in with this brochure about their training models and it was a waste of my time". How refreshing! I recommend you don't lead with your marketing collateral. Instead, tailor any collateral based on what you've learned from the client. Personalised collateral isn't damaging - it is the way forward.

Time to take note

A few years ago a work colleague shared a really valuable tip for how he took notes in client meetings. I've adopted it ever since and wanted to share it with you.

Prior to this revelation I took notes like I imagine most people take notes - writing down important (and sometimes un-important) information the client shared in a sequential manner. This was okay, but I found it quite difficult to reference my notes effectively during (and after) the meeting.

What I learned from my colleague was structure. He suggested I divide my note paper into 4 quadrants: 1 - for general information; 2 - for issues/concerns/ problems the client shared; 3 - for needs and agreed next steps/actions; 4 - for the decision process and decision criteria (more on this in chapters 5 and 6). By structuring my notes into sections they became easy to reference in the meeting, summarising was simple as was clarifying agreed actions at the end. Give it a go!

Chapter 5:

Value is more than just price

"An adventure is only an inconvenience rightly considered. An inconvenience is only an adventure wrongly considered."

- G. K. Chesterton

Win on price; lose on relationship

Some companies choose to win work by quoting a low price, but then finding ways to increase the price over the course of the project. I don't like it. I feel cheated. They may have won the work on price, but they have lost the relationship.

I recently did a house renovation. When I pressed my builder to reduce his price he replied "James, I could easily agree to your lower price to win the work and then, over the course of the renovations explain that X and Y has cost more than budgeted, and get you back to my original quote. But I don't work that way. I prefer to tell you what it's going to cost you and manage the project to this number to avoid any surprises". Personally I liked this approach and the 'certainty' it created - you rarely get that, especially with builders.

We all come up against competitors who try to win work by quoting low prices with no intention of sticking to them. When this happens you need to open the customer's eyes to this (in a nice way). It's important they are comparing apples with apples, not just fruit in general.

Wanting to buy or needing to sell?

Here's a question for you: do you think you would achieve a better price if:

A – you were needing to sell your services to a client, or

B – a client was keen to buy your services?

Hopefully you've gone with B. The more a client wants to buy from you the greater opportunity you have to charge a higher price. On the contrary, the more you're needing to sell to them, the more likely you'll need to discount. So instead of selling yourself/your services in your sales meetings, get the client wanting to buy from you. How? Go to every meeting with a view to 'teach' the client something new (giving not selling), don't talk about you/your company until the client asks you to, and ask questions and really listen to the answers. Just because your competitors are out there selling doesn't mean your clients aren't wanting to buy.

Never give something for nothing

When was the last time you won a sale without having to discount? Clients are forever challenging us on price, mainly because negotiating on price has become the norm. And our acceptance to say "okay" without getting anything in return simply fuels this dysfunctional practice.

The simple rule is never give something for nothing. Never give the same service/product, same people, same timeframes, same value-adds at just a lower price. Such concessions on price simply convince the customer they were right to beat us up in the first place, and so they always will. The only recourse is for us to artificially raise our price so it's ok when they beat us up, and so reinforce the process.

If you have to reduce price, get value in return - perhaps agreement not to tender/pitch for the work, a commitment of volume of work, early payment or payment in full by the customer, access to other decision makers etc.
It's time to get creative when negotiating on price.

Negotiate your way to the front

You have just read that if you're going to drop your price, get something in return. Perhaps there is an alternative before you look at dropping price. How about maintaining price and offering more of something else? We all seem so caught up in the 'price war' these days that we often forget everything else in our toolbox. What else do you have to negotiate with beside price?

I would recommend you prepare thoroughly before any negotiation to give yourself the best chance of success. Define the variables (price is only one) that are negotiable and map out the the parameters you're prepared to negotiate to and what concessions you want in return. Many people talk of "win-win" outcomes and I am a big believer that that's the only way to a mutually beneficial relationship.

How you negotiate matters most to clients

I remember going to China for the first time. A friend of mine who lives there gave me some good advice before I left - "if you go to the markets, make sure you are very friendly when you negotiate". At the markets I remember watching some westerners being arrogant, defiant or generally unpleasant to the locals and the negotiations falling apart, with both parties cursing the other. I was grateful for my friend's advice.

It made me realise that HOW you approach a negotiation makes a big difference to the eventual outcome. Being unpleasant doesn't help anyone. Most sales in my business are long term deals, not short term or one-off transactions, so I am of the view that how I act in the negotiation phase is a good indicator of what I will be like to work with. Keep it friendly!

Learning the decision criteria

"We've won it, we've won it, we've won it". And then we lost it! When my business partner debriefed with the client as to why we lost it, they told us that whilst they liked us they had decided to use someone they had used previously - and we thought they were no longer in the frame!

We learned an important lesson here. Because of the constant access we were given to the various decision makers and their friendliness towards us, we dropped our guard and with it some of the standard things we do. We made too many assumptions, especially around our competitors. We didn't ask the question: "who else are you considering?" We also failed to question the client about their decision criteria - the key factors for choosing one provider versus another. If we'd learned this, we would have better understood our chances of winning or losing...and avoided an unpleasant ending!

You don't have to drop price to win the deal

My wife and I recently renovated. We needed an architect to design the plans and so we met with three architects, all of whom came highly recommended. We were happy with all of them, so I called the one with the cheapest quote. I mentioned I was keen to use him, but I had a slightly cheaper option (sorry!), and asked if he would he be able to reduce his price to get the work. He instantly gave me a further 10% off. The fact is he was already the cheapest option and he would have won the work without any further discount, but I felt it was worth asking the question. Clients often do the same and so my advice is you don't always need to discount when asked. Clients ask about price because they want comfort they are getting a fair price, not because they always want to negotiate. I'd start by justifying my price rather than reducing it and hold onto my dollars.

Don't always believe you're too expensive

"I'm sorry, but you were just more expensive than the other company." I'm sure we have all heard this before! No one likes losing, but losing on price is probably the easiest to take and the easiest to rationalise. And here lies the problem.

It's not only the easiest for us to accept, it's also the easiest for clients to give - it's impossible to argue against, it's not personal (unlike "we didn't like you" or "we don't trust your company"), and it implies if you had been slightly cheaper you would have won. Clients unfortunately abuse the "you're too expensive" line and so it becomes a smoke screen for other factors. Unless you probe behind price and into the real reasons why you lost, you will continue to lose again and again. The moral is don't always believe what you're told.

A fair deal, not necessarily the cheapest deal

When was the last time a client asked you to increase your price instead of decrease it? Bizarrely it has happened to me twice this year. Perhaps I just got lucky, or perhaps it's an endorsement that I've chosen my clients well. All I know is that I really want my clients to succeed and I'm grateful that my clients seem to feel the same towards me. This seems a healthy relationship and relates to my ethos of being "mutually beneficial". When you have joint interest the pricing discussion no longer focuses on finding the lowest price, but the fair price, where both parties feel they are getting good value. How do find more of these clients? You need to uncover them during the sales process. Talk to them about the future, "12 months from now…", about what success looks like for them and what a successful relationship is in their eyes. You will quickly spot the ideal client.

Chapter 6:

Presenting and pitching (and generally creating some fizz!)

"We cannot direct the wind, but we can control the sails."

- Unknown

If you're not talking about your company, who is?

What is your answer to "Why should I choose you/your company?" I have found clients often think this but often don't ask it. But I guarantee they ask themselves the question when they are reviewing your proposal against a competitor's. You need to help them with this decision, which means addressing the "why you/your company" question. If the client doesn't ask the question, raise it. If they happen to ask the question, make sure you have a great answer, not an answer similar to your competitor. Probably not one that marketing gave you. You need a different answer, one that stands you apart - a differentiator.

Take some time this week to work on your response...and then try it out with clients.

Give the client what they want to hear

It's all about relevance. I'm sure you have lots of great things to say about yourself and your company, but is it relevant to this particular client? Most clients will have a reasonable understanding as to how they will decide which supplier/product to go with. I call this their 'decision criteria' - the criteria they will assess all suppliers/products against.

Typically the supplier/product that best aligns with these criteria wins. Often the biggest challenge when it comes to pitching is that the sales person doesn't know this criteria and ends up guessing. I recommend in order to give the client what they want, you need to establish the decision criteria before you deliver your presentation. Questions about the decision process and decision criteria are great questions to ask in the early sales meetings. Add them to your list now.

If the client thinks you're different, you are!

Even when you're not! Yes, differentiation comes down to the client's perception rather than reality. So even when your company, your product or you aren't any different to those of a competitor, you just need to make the client think you're different. Whilst many companies would like to think their product is better, their people are better and they are different, it's becoming rare in today's market. Even first to market no longer gives long term differentiation, with products and solutions being quickly replicated.

So find out what are the most important aspects for every client and overlay your capabilities to these. Even though competitors may have similar capabilities, if you stress them and your competitors don't, you are different.

Better the devil you know...

Imagine you're pursuing a new client. They haven't bought from you before, they haven't worked with you before and they haven't used your company before. In essence they have no real way of knowing what it would be like to be a 'client' of yours. They may be asking themselves "Are you full of hot air? Are you over-promising? Will you really be better than our current supplier?" Clients naturally fear the worst and think 'better the devil they know than the one they don't'.

I think the best indication of what it would be like to work with you is what you do during your business development interactions. Recent research (from the Sales Executive Council) supports this, indicating the client's experience during the sales process is the biggest factor in the purchasing decision - even more so than price. So actually YOU are the difference!

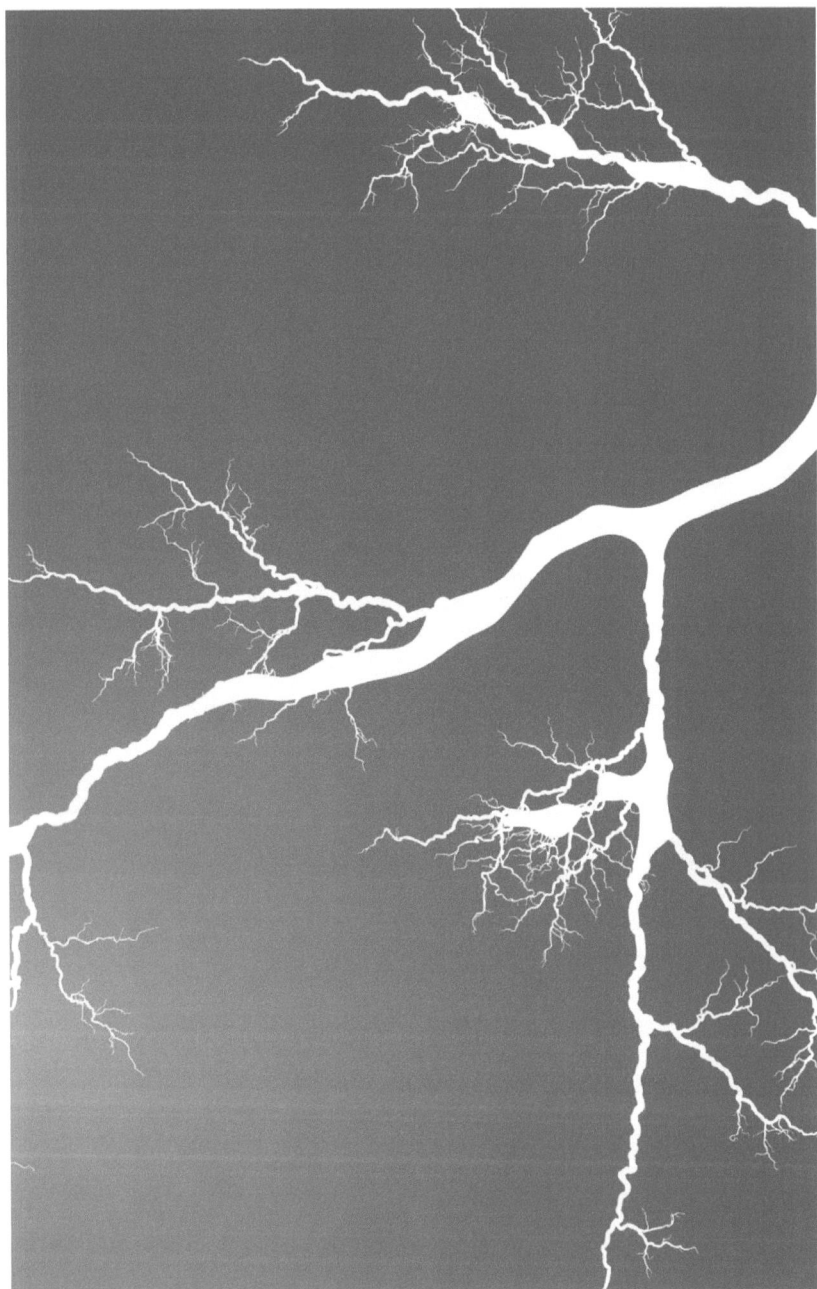

Live and die by the Q & A session

I've seen many good presentations destroyed in the Question and Answer (Q&A) session. The control and confidence shown in the presentation disappears and is replaced with nervousness and a sweaty brow...
When I coach on pitching, I spend a lot of time on prepping for Q&A. Thinking in advance of possible questions the client may ask and how you should respond is invaluable. Following the mantra (plan for the worst and hope for the best) I suggest you identify the questions you'd least like the client to ask you - probing around your weaknesses, your competitor's strengths, your proposed pricing etc. Now rehearse your responses, perhaps even in a role play situation with a colleague or manager. Knowing you're ready to handle the toughest questions gives a real confidence boost to the whole presentation.

Three reasons to pick me...

You have rehearsed, you're feeling confident and prepared...and then the client ambushes you. They take control of the meeting from the moment you walk in. They no longer want to hear what you had planned to say; they want to dominate the meeting and determine the direction it takes.

Whilst this might seem extreme, I have seen it happen quite a few times - especially when the client is sitting through multiple vendor presentations and is getting frustrated at hearing the same pitch over and over again. "Let's just cut to the chase" they think. Whilst you can be as prepared as you'll ever be, you shouldn't forget the power of **three key messages**. I would encourage you to decide what they are, then introduce them at the start, during the presentation and in your summary. Even when ambushed the three messages will shine though, and it might be all that the client remembers.

Another death by PowerPoint

When are you next giving a presentation? If it's not in the next 30 minutes, you still have time. Time to define what you ask for, time to make it simpler, more powerful, more memorable and more effective. That's the purpose of presentations after all!
Our default is PowerPoint...millions of which are delivered every day, the majority of which fail to fulfill their potential. Why, because they're dull, text heavy and fail to engage the audience.

Good presentations make an emotional sale. They tell your ideas and your point of view. Your slides are your glamorous assistant, catching the eye of the audience and making your presentation memorable days and weeks later.

So stop giving the same presentation before it kills again. It's time to make changes.

Is not what you say, but HOW you say it

In my experience, when faced with a pitch or presentation, most people spend all their time working out what they are going to say...and spend no time considering HOW they will deliver it. Many of you have probably heard the statistics that only 7% of our communication is through the words we use (verbal), 38% is down to the tone, pitch, speed of what we say (vocal) and the remaining 55% down to body language (visual).

Whether you agree with the exact percentages or not, I hope we can all agree that we shouldn't simply focus on what words we say when presenting. Think where you can add a pause to create an effect. Rehearse your speed (most of us need to slow down). Practice giving out positive body language - use some (not too many) hand gestures and even a smile goes a long way to getting the audience on your side!

Brevity. The power of being concise

Mark Twain said "I didn't have time to write you a short letter, so I wrote you a long one instead." He's right but time gets the better of us and consequently both clients and us suffer. Expecting clients to read through your 80 page proposal or sit through your waffly presentation will stifle your success.

It is hard to be brief and to the point, yet when we are it stands out. When a client stipulates our proposal can only be 5 pages long, we manage it. Yet why can't we replicate this when clients don't insist on it? Just imagine the surprise on a client's face (surprise of joy not disappointment, I assure you!) when they see a ten-page document instead of everyone else's novel. So next time you put pen to paper (or finger to keyboard), just remember these words: brevity...

Leader of the pack

"Many hands make light work", yet "too many cooks spoil the broth". At times proverbs can be confusing!

Whenever you are presenting with others, you need to act as a team. And all teams have leaders - just look at any sports team. Having a leader / captain has benefits for your team and for the client. The leader should open the presentation, introduce the team members and share the agenda, thereby providing structure from the outset. The leader doesn't have to do all the talking, but should direct 'traffic' throughout the presentation, facilitate the answering of any questions that arise and ensure the audience is engaged. Having a leader and clear roles for people in the team gives everyone focus. To the client you look cohesive, you look like a team, you look organised and there is clear structure. If I was in the client's shoes, you're the sort of team I'd be picking!

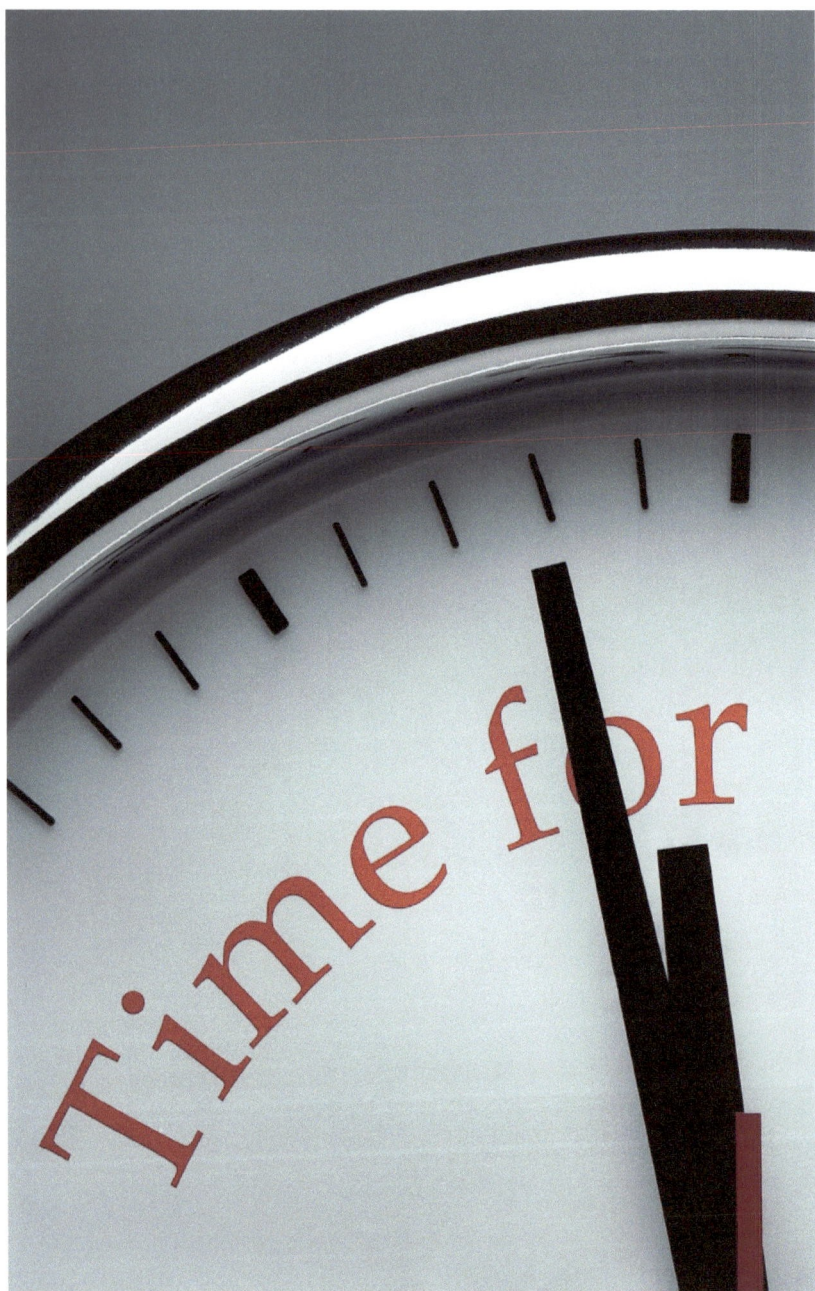

Watching the clock

No matter how much time we are given by the client to present, it's never enough. When faced with running out of time, some people simply ignore it and hope the client doesn't 'time them out'. Others start speaking faster and faster in the hope to get through everything they want to say. With a bit of forward thinking you can take time pressure out of the equation. How?

1. Do a timed rehearsal of your presentation. This will give you a good indication if you need to reduce the amount of content you have

2. Decide in advance which parts of the presentation you can skip or shorten if you become short of time. Planning for this scenario will give you confidence if it actually eventuates

3. Divide your presentation into time slots. This will enable you from the outset to see how you are tracking against the plan

4. Be realistic. One-hour for a pitch only equates to 30 minutes of presenting, 5 mins for introductions, 15-20 minutes for Q&A etc. Better to underestimate!

Take a seat...or should I stand?

I often get asked "should I sit down or stand up for this presentation?" There are no hard and fast rules, but here are my suggestions:

1. Be guided by how many people are in the room. My tipping point is 6-8 people. Anything above this, I prefer to stand up

2. It depends how formal you want to make the presentation. Sitting down creates a more informal environment than standing up

3. Are you wanting to deliver 'thought leadership' and position yourself as an 'expert', or would you prefer to have more of a discussion with the audience? It is often easier to have a discussion sitting at the table and as 'one of them'

4. If you want to use slides (e.g. PowerPoint) it is better to stand up and engage with the audience. If you are sitting down, the audience will look at the slides and not at you, which isn't ideal.

5. If you're ever in doubt, ask the client.

Chapter 7:

When the going gets tough

"When our wagon gets stuck in the mud, God is much more likely to assist the man who gets out to push than the man who merely raises his voice in prayer—no matter how eloquent the oration."

— Dieter F. Uchtdorf

Beware the 'zone of indifference'

Do you have a favorite pub/restaurant you frequent? Mine is a pub in Sydney. I go there once or twice a fortnight and always (always) have the fillet steak. Nothing else. Other places serve steak, but I'm not interested. Without even going there and trying them, I'm not interested. Great steaks have made me loyal to this place, so that's where I go.

It's not the same with pizza though. No restaurant has earned my loyalty yet. I'll go from place to place giving them a go. I'll be persuaded by special offers, by discounts, by referrals. This is the last place you want your customers to be - what I call the zone of indifference. Here there is little/zero loyalty to you. So look at your favorite pub/restaurant, work out what they do to gain your loyalty and emulate it.

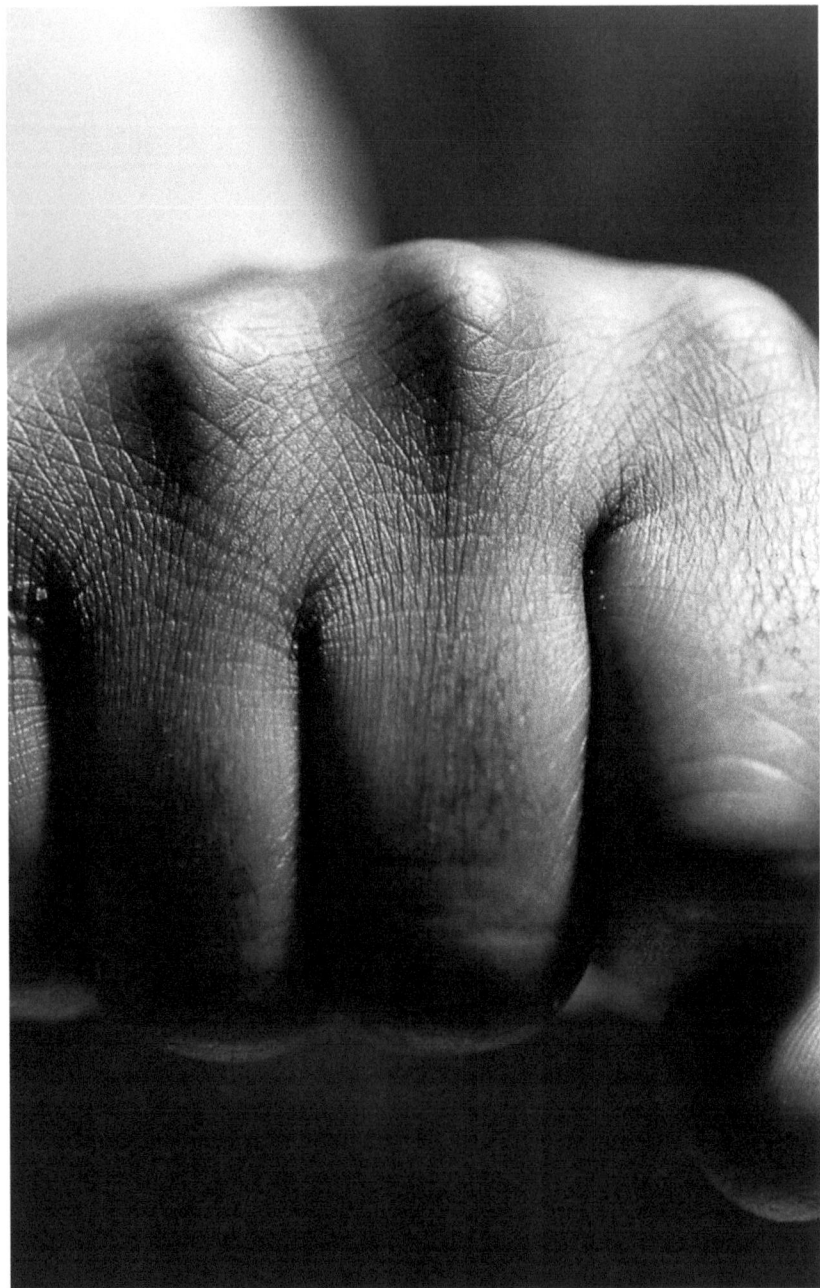

"The hot seat": avoiding death by questions!

If you have ever walked into a client meeting and been bombarded by question after question, you'll know why I'm calling it the "hot seat". I imagine it's like boxing against someone with a much longer reach than you...who hits you with their jab time and time again and you can't get a shot in at all. Well, I have a solution (to the questioning not the boxing!):

When asked a question, don't immediately jump to respond. There is often an opportunity to postpone your response by asking a question yourself thereby ensuring your eventual response is more targeted. For example if I was asked "why should we choose you?" I'd answer "That depends. I may or may not be the best option for you - what exactly are you looking for?" This buys you time, but also gets the client talking - and their engagement will get them to drop their guard.

Getting the ego out of the room

Selling to people with big ego's is always a challenge. They want you to know they are in charge, they are the client and their ideas and opinions are better than yours (and anyone else's in the room!). It's a tough gig! Fighting fire with fire is rarely the answer, and I have found the best way to deal with big ego's is to play to them, at least to some extent. They will have a view and opinion, so I think it's better to get it on the table; they will want the meeting to run in a particular way, so it's better to ask. My best advice is to engage them and work with them, not against them. Share your agenda for the meeting but make a big point of telling them it's their meeting and ask them what they want from it. This makes it feel like it is their meeting. Instead of letting them dominate the meeting, ask them lots of questions, solicit their views and opinions and get their input throughout. You need them engaged not crashing the party at the end. As George Bernard Shaw said "never wrestle with pigs. You both get dirty and the pig likes it."

Always look on the bright side of sales

I will always remember my first sales manager telling me that "nurses get sore feet, accountants get sore eyes, and sales people get no's". I admit it is easier said than done, but it's true - we are never going to win every sales opportunity; we are never going to 'click' with every potential client we meet so we should get realistic! Add to this the fact that some clients don't actually make the right purchasing decision sometimes - they stick with their current provider whom they are very unhappy with or they choose someone that you know is not as good as you. Yes, just because they are the client doesn't mean they are smart!
So don't dwell on the loss. Learn from it and move on, quickly. One boss I had would literally walk out of the client's building, announce them as "idiots" and then ask "who are we seeing next?". I always marveled at his positive attitude!

Go with it. Don't fight it.

Unlike boxing, various forms of martial arts teach you to use the opponent's power to your advantage. Whilst I don't advocate fighting with your clients, it's an interesting metaphor when dealing with client's objections. The last thing you want to do when client's pushback is to resist and pushback yourself. You'll get nowhere and the client will walk away. Time to stop fighting it and instead go with it.

Firstly, look at objections in a positive not negative light. Whilst you don't want constant objections, some are actually good. They indicate the client is at least listening and considering what you're saying. The phrase "clients who don't object rarely buy" springs to mind and it's probably true.

Secondly, objections are often misunderstandings. The best approach is to listen to the client and better understand their concern before you respond. Acknowledge their concern, then clarify exactly what the concern is. Only when you understand their perspective can you really respond.

Chapter 8:

Teaming around sales

"Teamwork is the ability to work together toward a common vision. The ability to direct individual accomplishments toward organisational objectives. It is the fuel that allows common people to attain uncommon results."

- Unknown

Team GB

It's important that we get one thing straight: while I still cannot shake my English accent no one should ever doubt that my sporting allegiances lie first and foremost with Australia. That said, there is an important lesson here when we look at the performance of "Team GB".

In contrast to Australia, Team GB won many unexpected gold medals at London 2012. It seemed to be that simply donning the Team GB tracksuit guaranteed athletes a podium finish. The question remains where did such a powerful surge of momentum come from?

The answer I believe is in Team GB's attitude towards success. Anytime an athlete won a medal the entire team celebrated and rejoiced in the individual's achievement. Turning personal victories into shared success created a strong spirit of positivity and the belief that anything was possible.

You can start a similar momentum in your company's sales efforts by tapping into this spirit through two easy steps. Firstly, build momentum and positivity by taking the time to acknowledge and celebrate the sales wins of your colleagues. It only takes a few minutes to send a quick email to a colleague when they've won a tender or achieved a great outcome. Secondly, you can be more forthright in sharing your company's successes when you are speaking to clients. Never underestimate the reassurance clients take from working with a company that is "going places".

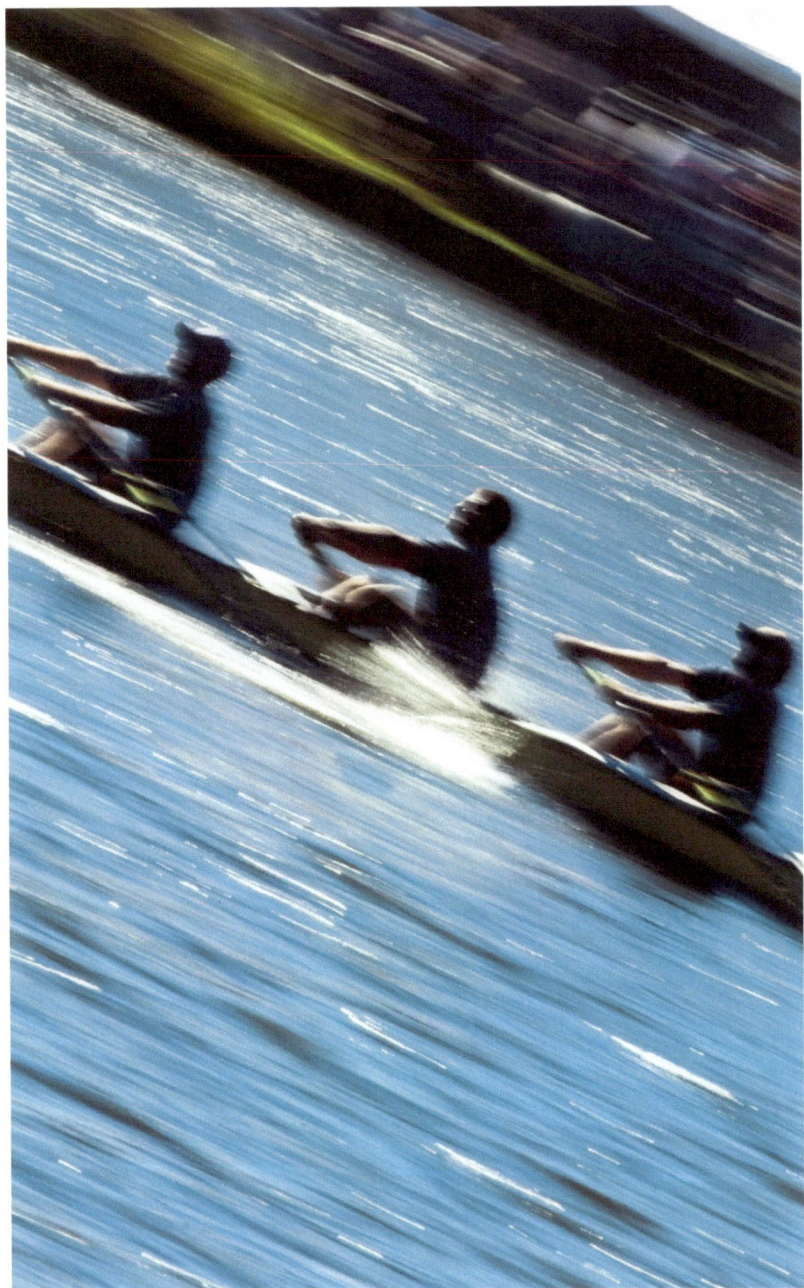

Teaming around opportunities

Whatever industry you're working in, I believe there is an opportunity to team more. Collaboration is the war-cry in most organisations these days! I personally never understand why it is often done so badly and so infrequently. Getting together with like-minded colleagues to **brainstorm ideas to take to clients** seems obvious to me. Leveraging what colleagues in your other offices are doing with their clients also seems obvious...yet they rarely speak to each other let alone share ideas. Find out what they are talking to their clients about, what presentations have they have recently delivered and which type of clients you can replicate this with. When you team around business development, particularly around ideas to take to clients, everyone wins. So come on, what is stopping you from instigating this in your company RIGHT NOW? Join the teaming revolution.

The closer you get to the action, the more you'll see

And the more you see, the more you'll understand. This is the simple rule to watching sport, and it applies to business as well. That's why collaboration is so important in business today. Avoid silo-mentality and instead TEAM around opportunities and ideas to take to clients. Get other people involved with your clients, such as asking more junior members of the team to join the sales meetings or other parts of your company.

Perhaps listening more to your clients and finding out their priorities and their needs will provide the insight of who to involve from your company. Once someone starts this process, reciprocity kicks in and momentum builds. The challenge however is finding someone to kick-start this initiative. Could it be you?

Lesson learned from a Bondi surfer

I recently had a surfing lesson at Bondi beach. I left better than when I started, but that's not saying much! A few week's later I attended a sales conference. The team building activity happened to be surfing. There were 30 of us but only 2 surf coaches, so I decided to help 'coach' my colleagues rather than surf myself. And it worked - I got everyone standing and riding a wave!

My question is why doesn't this happen more in sales? Why don't we help and support each other more? My surfing experience taught me that you don't have to be an expert at something in order to coach others. An understanding of basic principles is often enough, so offer to help a colleague prepare for a client meeting or an important presentation. Remember, what goes around comes around.

Internal sales meetings need a touch of Jose

Let's be honest. The majority of internal sales meetings are a complete waste of time. That's because too much time is spent looking backwards (in the rear view mirror), not forwards, people arrive late or not at all, the meetings often get cancelled, everyone is on their Blackberry/iPhone and so on.

It is time to take some inspiration from soccer. I'm sure half-time talks are not like internal sales meetings. Imagine sitting in on Jose Mourinho's (the famous soccer coach of Chelsea and Real Madrid and known as "the chosen one") half-time team talk - it would be short, sharp, effective, morale boosting, motivational, inspiring and forward looking. Whether 2-0 ahead or behind, Jose would focus on the 2nd half. After all, it's the 2nd half that will determine the winners and losers. Time to take a leaf out of Jose's book.

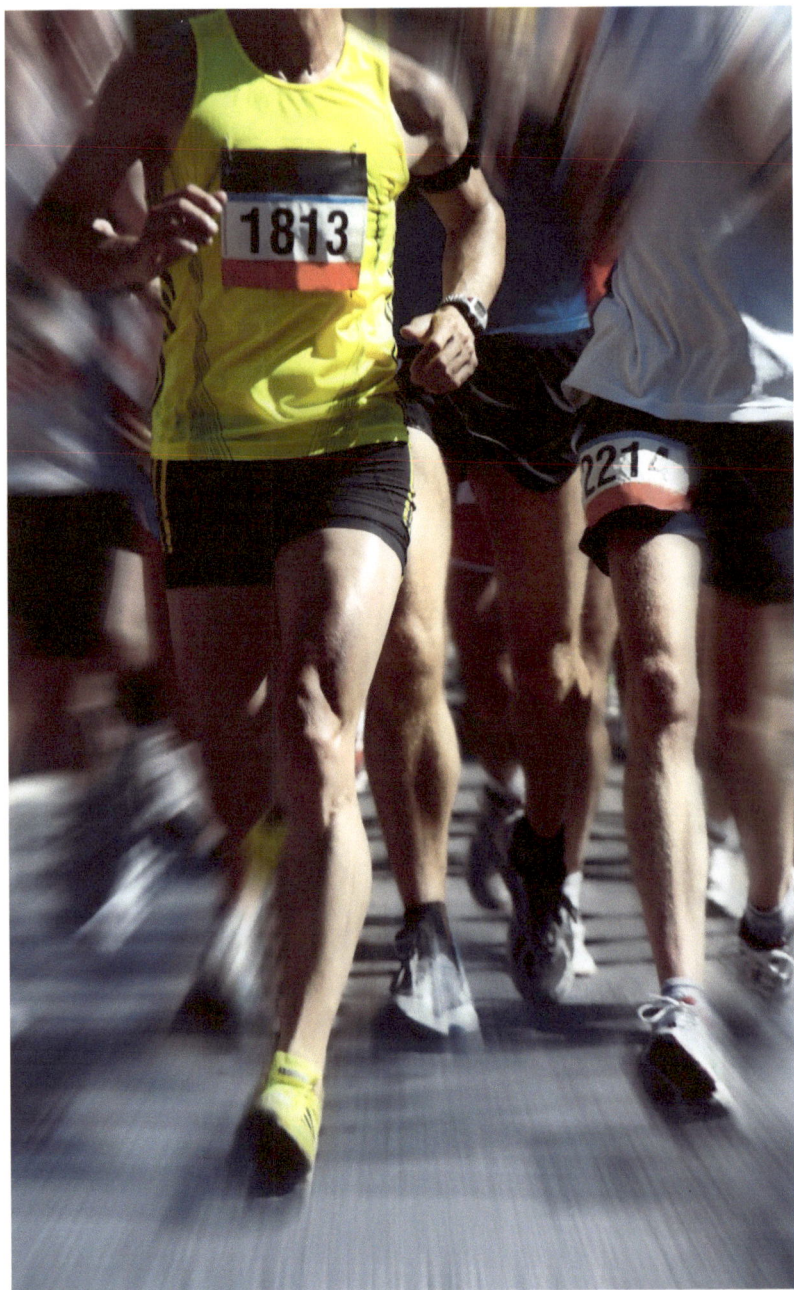

Going the distance - with a helping hand

A friend of mine runs marathons. He keeps setting himself PBs (personal bests) to achieve. In one marathon he was flying at the half-way point, but by 28 kms he was hurting and by 36 kms was really struggling and questioning whether he would finish. In the spirit of marathon running, a fellow runner, also hurting, reached out and said "let's finish this together". Between them (and another person they picked up in similar circumstances) they motivated themselves to the finish line. Sales targets are a little like marathons. We often have the skills to succeed, but there are times we'll need the support of others to reach the finish line. Take a look around you. Which colleagues are hurting at the moment? Who needs the pat on the back, the word in their ear and the "let's finish this together"?

Introducing colleagues into relationships

"Can you get me a meeting with your client?" was a question I was often asked in my consulting days. I think requests like this is one of the hardest aspects of being a 'relationship manager' (RM) for a key account. As the RM you don't want to be calling in favours to grant access for others. Surely there is a better way? And there is. I believe the responsibility for getting access doesn't simply lie with the RM, but actually lies more with the person wanting access. Why should the client meet with them? What have they got to say to the client that the client would find of value? What is the compelling reason? Cross selling into existing clients requires an element of 'new business' mentality. In the majority of instances there is another provider servicing their needs in this other area, so they have no perceived need to see you.

So again, the question is what have you got to give?

Selling is a contact sport

Technology has done a lot to help marketeers and sales people. Linked In, e-marketing, video conferencing, Skype and Google Hangout to name a few. The challenge I see is now "over use" of technology at the expense of old fashioned methods. Email seems to have replaced phone calls as well as much internal face to face collaboration. Although I'm an early adopter when it comes to technology, I still see selling as a "contact sport".

Relationships need to be built in person - just look at how few long distance relationships survive if you want evidence. So before you hit "send" on the next email, consider if a phone call would be better. Before you email someone in your own office, could you walk around and see them in person? The personal touch matters and whilst emails are often the quick and easy option, they are rarely the best.

Chapter 9:

The 1% Difference

"If I'd have asked my customers what they'd have wanted, they'd have said a faster horse"

- Henry Ford

Tiger's 1% difference generated 86% more!

Let me take you back a few years, to the time Tiger Woods was undisputed world Number 1. One year he reportedly earned 86% more prize money than Phil Mickelson, the world number 2. Interestingly the cause of this massive difference in pay-packets was less than 1% difference in shots per round. 1% meant that Tiger and Phil were separated by less than one shot each day, yet the difference in rewards was astronomical. Irrespective of whether you are a fan of golf (or even Tiger), you can probably marvel at the difference we can all yield from operating at peak level.

My challenge to you is this - what is going to give you the 1% difference over your competition?

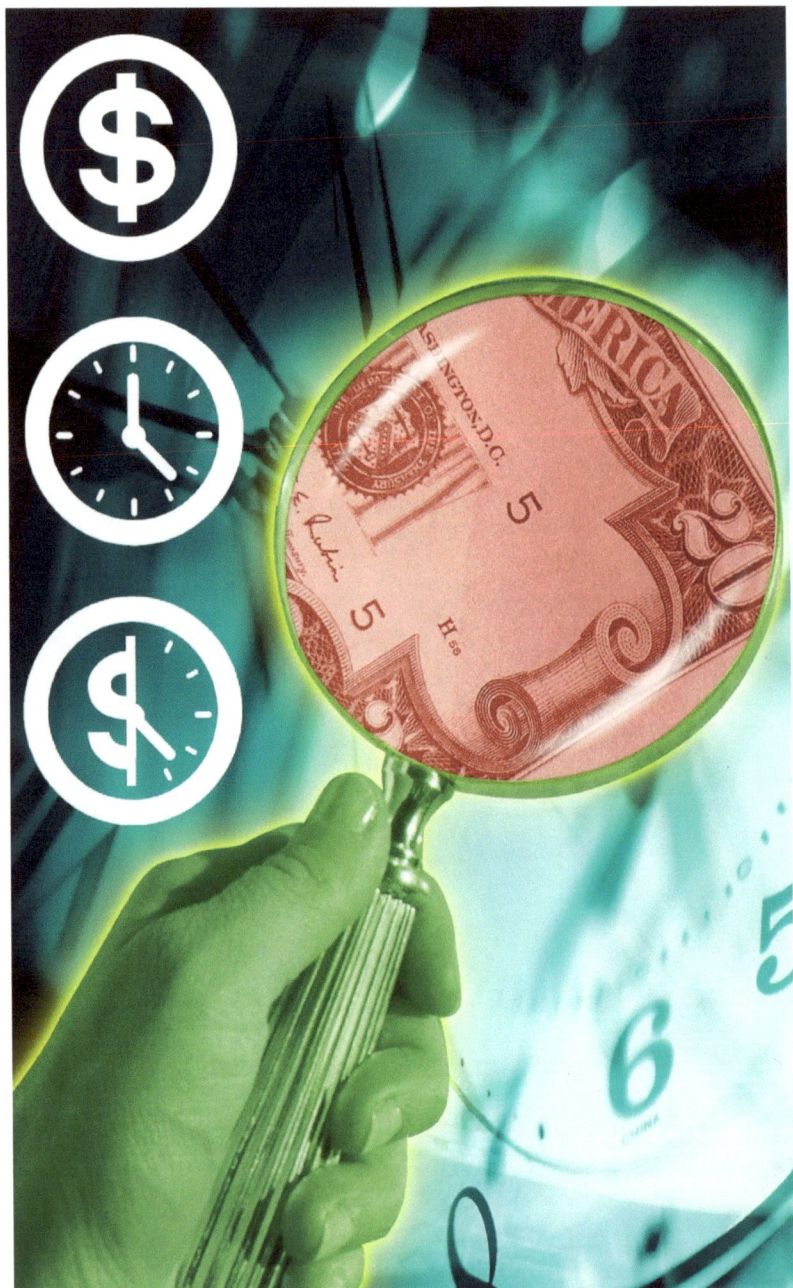

Time is money. 1% is the difference

A few years back Yvon Chouinard, the founder of Patagonia (the outdoor clothing company) decided to contribute 1% of his company's annual revenue ($22m that year) to support the environment, as well as influencing a further 250 other companies to do the same. It was his 1% difference.

Now I'm not after your money, I'm after your time. The most common reason sales people don't do as well as they could is down to poor preparation - for the call, the meeting, the pitch, the proposal, the networking event etc. Yet selling requires preparation. So I ask that you give an extra 1% of your time (maybe 30 minutes a week) to really prepare for a meeting. My hope is that once you've experienced the difference this 1% planning time makes you'll readily give more. But don't procrastinate with your planning - you miss 100% of the shots you don't take after all!

Learning from today's librarian

The crusty old person wearing the grey cardigan, protecting all the books and enforcing silence? That was the librarian of the past.

Today's librarian isn't a clerk who happens to work at a library, but is a data hound, a guide, a sherpa and a teacher. Today's librarian is the interface between all the data at our fingertips and our clients. Today's librarian uses their great knowledge of the client, their business and their needs and meshes this with their company's expertise/products. Today's librarians are today's sales people and I think this approach can create a 1% difference.

All of a sudden grey cardigans are cool. I want one!

Strive to be different

Many say "don't fix it if it isn't broken". I say "how boring! Don't fix it isn't fantastic. Now that's better!" After all, when you're green you grow, when you're ripe you rot!

People love habits. It means they don't have to think. Habits can be problematic though - hard to break and keeping us oblivious of the need to change. Instead, I wave the flag of continuous improvement. Every week I take a different route on my Vespa on my way to work, in the attempt to find a better, quicker, less stressful or more enjoyable route.

It can be the same with sales. We do the same thing over and over again. We conduct our meetings in the same way. We pitch the same way. So how can we expect a different outcome? We can't. So make a change and take a risk. Spend next week looking at the things you do regularly and look for improvements. Change the way you are on the phone, the questions you ask clients, how you pitch, how you network at client events...this change could be your 1% difference!

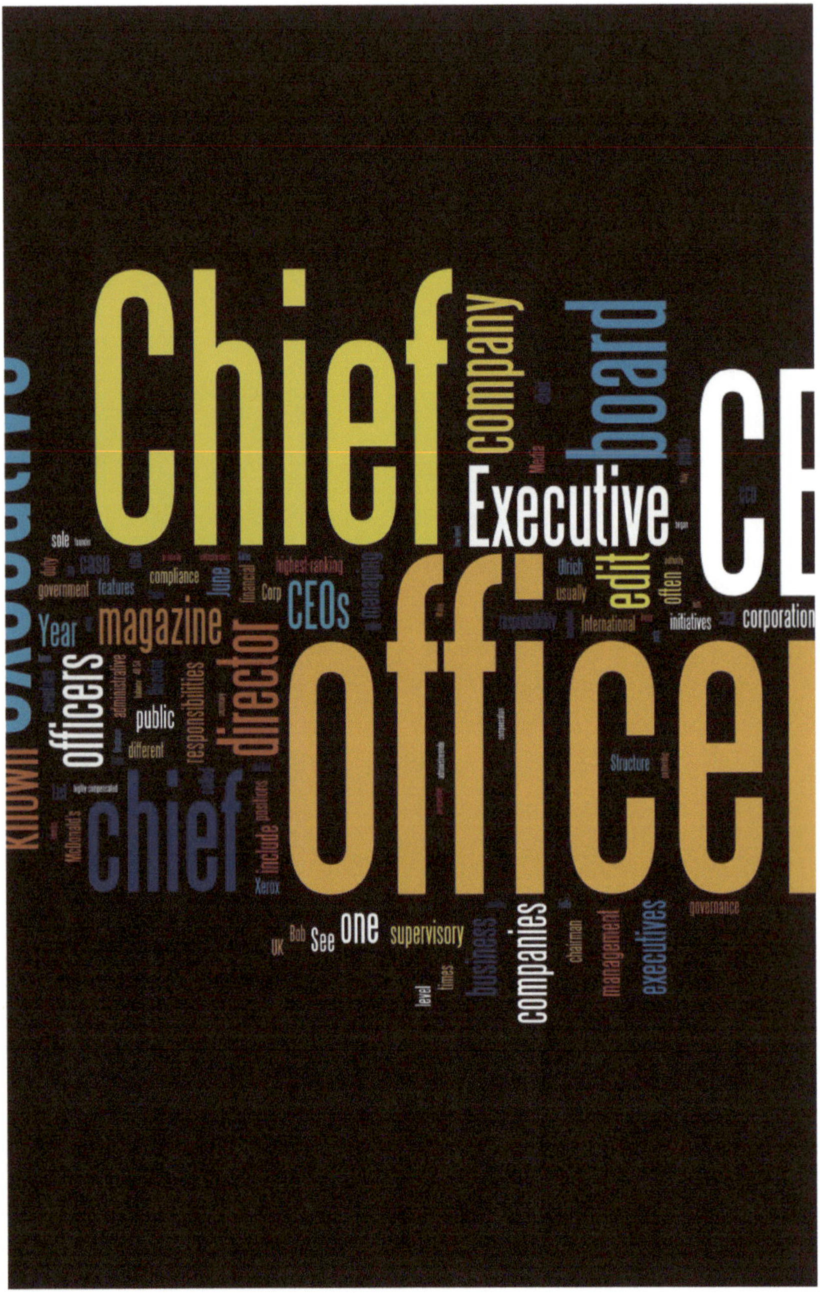
Chief
Executive
company
board
officers
chief
director
magazine
CEOs
Year
public
different
responsibilities
administrative
corporation
initiatives
International
usually
often
edit
Ulrich
compliance
June
features
government
case
sole
duty
highest-ranking
Corp
financial
managing
Structure
Xerox
include
positions
McDonald's
known
one
See
Bob
UK
supervisory
business
companies
chairman
management
executives
governance
times
level

The CXO

Every year I make a point of reading Miller Heiman's annual Study into 'Sales Best Practices'. The publication highlights the key aspects separating world-class sales organisations from the also-rans by pinpointing the sales activities commonly found amongst the top performers. 2012 didn't disappoint with one activity standing out in my mind – the importance of senior executive engagement.

This year Miller Heiman concentrated on the number, and quality, of relationships companies have with the executive levels of their "strategic" clients. In addition they investigated the frequency of dialog between the company and their client's senior managers. Startlingly only 38% of 'average' rated organisations could claim to have executive level relationships with whom they regularly spoke. In comparison, 96% of 'world-class' organisations had mastered this initiative.

Getting the attention of the C-suite can be hard however I urge you to target more executive level meetings as part of your 1% difference.

Painting the town red

You may be interested to learn that each year Disneyland uses over 19,000 litres of paint to maintain the clean appearance of the park. That's a lot of paint...and a lot of painting! A good appearance not only impresses new visitors to the park, but also those loyal customers returning year after year.

So my question is what's your equivalent of paint? What are you doing to make a great impression with new and existing clients? Relationship check-ins and client listening programs are obviously part of the solution, but what about making a big effort around responsiveness, around picking up the phone rather than an over-reliance on email, around notifying the client of issues **before** they call you, around an instant response to concerns raised by the client and so on.

In my view there is a lot of painting to be done. What's your colour? Ours is red so pick something different!

Feel your way to success

I stopped playing guitar when I was 13. It wasn't that I was bad, it was more that my singing was bad. I'd sing along as I played, but as soon as I heard anyone walking nearby I'd stop and "tune" the guitar out of embarrassment. So it was my bad voice that killed my guitar career in the end! I never really felt comfortable with my guitar anyway. In those days every guitar you bought was right-handed. I was left-handed, and whilst it was easy enough to change the strings over, you never got a true feel what a guitar was actually like when you tried one in the shop. Apparently that's what guitarists will tell you is the difference between a good and a bad guitar – not the quality of the guitar but how it feels for you.

As a client choosing a provider there are many comparisons. Of course quality of product/service is important, but feel could be the deciding factor. Some times we get so wrapped up selling our quality that we forget about the feel. So next time you're in front of a client, really work hard to ensure it feels right for them and you. If you're in doubt, don't be afraid to ask.

Make it count

The 2012 US Open tennis final was incredibly tight. After four and a half grueling sets of tennis both Andy Murray and Novak Djokovic had won exactly the same number of points - 154.

Murray eventually triumphed to win his first 'Slam' and the question was posed "in such a close match what made the difference?" The answer lies not in the total effort expended but in who won the most important points.

Watching the match I couldn't help but relate it to sales and our efforts to win and grow clients. Many companies have to offer 'value-adds' as part of the pitch to win work. I fear these value adds have come to mean "free stuff" and our reaction is the more free things we can give clients the better.

Instead, you should promote the less is more principle. Concentrate on identifying the important investments you can make in the client's business not on the amount of freebies you are offering. This way you have a greater chance of winning the important points and making the 1% difference.

It's not who you know, but who wants to know you

I have always bought into the concept that "it's not what you know, it's who you know". But recently I have been trying to take this concept one step further - it's no longer who you know, but more importantly who wants to know you.

For me it reinforces two key elements to building a strong network:

1. You need to give to your network more than you take from it; and
2. You need to be proactive rather than responsive.

Perhaps it's time to review your network and proactively look for ways to give: introductions you can make; giving your time to help others; recommending or endorsing someone on LinkedIn etc. I think you'll find giving is hugely rewarding.

One final thought

"They're not that different from you, are they? Same haircuts. Full of hormones, just like you. Invincible, just like you feel. The world is their oyster. They believe they're destined for great things, just like many of you, their eyes are full of hope, just like you.....if you listen real close, you can hear them whisper their legacy to you. Go on, lean in. Listen, you hear it? - - Carpe - - hear it? - - Carpe, carpe diem, seize the day boys, make your lives extraordinary."

- Robin Williams, Dead Poets Society

I hope you enjoyed reading the book. If you would like to comment on the book as a whole, particular chapters or certain stories, I would love to hear from you.

Please email your thoughts, comments or questions to:

whoisdoingwhothefavour@gmail.com

Alternatively, join us on Facebook - http://www.facebook.com/pages/Who-is-doing-who-the-favour/302447550279?ref=hl

I wish you all the very best

www.ingramcontent.com/pod-product-compliance
Lightning Source LLC
Chambersburg PA
CBHW042146220326
41599CB00003BB/7